OF FAMILY AND FAITH

Published by:

SA Catholic Online Books
59 Tom Brown Boulevard,
St Francis Bay 6312
Tel: +27(0)422941023
frank@sacatholiconline.org
www.sacatholiconline.org

Edited by: Frank Nunan
Cover, Book Design & Layout: Frank Nunan

ISBN: 978-0-6398103-0-0

OF FAMILY AND FAITH

BY

DOUG BOAKE

Dedication

Lynne, my wife,

and

Graeme, Bruce, Kevin and Trevor, our four sons

their wives

and

our grandchildren scattered all over the world

and

all future generations of Boakes

The proceeds from the sale of this book will go to The Douglas Boake Foundation for the promotion of social justice, entrepreneurial endeavors and the protection of the natural environment.

About the Author

Doug was born in Pietersburg (now Polokwane) in Limpopo at the outbreak of World War in 1939.

The family lived in Palapye, Bechuanaland Protectorate (now Botswana). He matriculated in 1957 at Pietersburg High School (now Capricorn High).

After qualifying as a Chartered Accountant in 1964, Doug started Boake Inc, a professional audit practice in Bedfordview.

The firm has been a member of BKR International, a leading global association of independent accounting and advisory firms for more than 20 years.

He and Lynne were married in 1966 and they have four sons and 12 grandchildren living in South Africa, the UK and the USA. In 2010, together with his brother Jock and his wife Moira, they travelled 17 000 km through the wilds of Africa to north of Nairobi in two Landrovers, when they were forced to return home because on terrorist attacks on travellers.

Doug has completed the Comrades Marathon, the Duzi Canoe Race and swum the Midmar Mile.

To date Doug and Lynne have undertaken four Caminos in Spain, Portugal and France, walking thousands of kms with fellow pilgrims all over the world.

He is a deacon at St Joseph's Catholic Parish in Primrose South Africa.

Acknowledgements

I am most grateful and indebted to Lori McDonald for her assistance and patience in getting this publication to its final stage.

To Frank Nunan for proof reading and his meticulous editorial work in making the publication a reality.

Doug Boake
19 October 2019.

Contents

Dedication iv

About the Author v

Acknowledgements vi

Preface x

Chapter 1   I Believe 1

Gospel of the New Covenant 4

Faith is Caught, Not Taught 7

Understanding the Eucharist 7

Meaning of Life 9

The Seven Sacraments 11

The Apostles' Creed 12

Mary Mother of God 15

Lourdes 17

Reconciliation 20

Chapter 2   Prayer 22

Simple Prayer 23

Our Father 26

Family Grace 29

Prayers to the Saints 31

Prayers to Mary, Mother of God 32

The Rosary 34

Stations of the Cross 34

One Solitary Life 36

Statues 37

Intercessory Prayer 38

Eucharistic Adoration 39

Mass 40

Chapter 3 Faith 46

Catholicism 46

Protestantism 53

*The Main Differences Between Catholicism
   and Protestantism* 56
Spiritual Reading 59
Never the Twain Shall Meet 60
The Ups and Downs of Faith 61
You'll Never Walk Alone 64
Footprints in the Sand 65
The Imitation of Christ 66
Rejoice and Be Glad 68
The Three Little Catholics of St Agapantha's 70
Noontime for the Church 74
The Diaconate 76
Proudly Catholic 87
Church Chuckle 88

Chapter 4 Parenting **89**

Preparation As Parents 89
Beginning In Awe 90
Parent Leadership 94
Kids in Trouble 95
The Consumerist Family: A Composite Picture 98
Parents Headed for Trouble 99
Children Headed for Trouble 101
Parenting Adult Children 104
The 'Transformation Years', 25 to 30 106
Hovering In The Background 107
IF 108
Counselling 110
Elements of Counselling 113

Chapter 5 Family Values **115**

Nothing Has Really Changed For Mankind 115
The Breakdown of Family Life 115
Marriage 115
Love 123
Birth Control 124

Abortion...125
Divorce..128
Annulment of Marriage..133
Addictions 135
Theology of the Body..141
Death...143
Growing Through the Years 145
Boake Family Genealogy 147
The Nuts and Bolts of Modern Family Life......................151
Social Media 157
Fourth Industrial Revolution - AI....................................157

Chapter 6 New Challenges In Retirement **161**
Facing Old Age 161
Happiness and Joy 162
How To Retire Happy 165
Taking Control of Your Life 168
Prayer of La Faba 174
Looking After Planet Earth 177

Chapter 7 Facing The End **182**
Our Ache for Earthly Immortality 182
Journey of the Spirit..183
Memories..184
Role Model 185
Cat's In The Cradle 187
Grateful for Professional Achievements...........................191
Bits And Pieces – An Old Accountant Recalls The Past..191
Walk the Talk..196
Temporary Crown 197
Final Prayer 197
Final Hymn...198

PREFACE

I suppose it is only natural that as the end draws near for your sojourn here on earth that you reflect back on the highs and lows of your life.

For most of us, these are bittersweet memories. But they needn't be if you see life as a journey each one of us must undertake. See it as experiencing life to the fullest.

You may feel that you have something to pass on to future generations from your personal experiences. Will they listen and benefit from this? I doubt it, for the simple reason that every new generation has a variety of excuses – times have changed, we are the new generation, that's old fashioned stuff, it didn't work in the past so it won't work now, and so the list goes on.

So they will have to find out the hard way for themselves, as we did. Hopefully, they have a soft landing!

Concern: Is There a God?

My concern for the future is that the vast majority of humans throughout history have grown up with questions like *"Is there a God?"* and *"What happens when people die?"*

Most people took comfort from being told, loudly and clearly, that death is not the end. But today many people say that death is the end, whilst fewer people are totally convinced otherwise. Many people, in one way or another, are sort of religious, but it is like an opt-in.

The thought of regular religious observances unnerves them because of peer pressure and the unsettling explanation offered: "No, it is something I have concluded-in-my-head", which seems to advance the implication that they think you should have concluded it too.

In one of the issues of his weekly column, *Final Reflections,* Fr Ron Rolheiser OMI explains why he believes in God. He is a well-known writer of our era and his explanations are perfectly logical to me. He gives food for thought about his fundamental belief in mankind since the beginning of creation.

Here is what he writes:

Today belief in God is often seen a naïveté. For many, believing in God is like believing in Father Christmas and the Easter Bunny – nice, something for the kids, a warm nostalgia or a bitter memory, but not something that's real, that stands up to hard scrutiny and indeed stands up to the dark doubts that sometimes linger below the surface of our faith.

Where, they ask, is there evidence that God exists?

A true apologetic (that is - a religious discipline of defending religious doctrines through systematic argumentation and discourse), I believe, needs at a point to be personal. So here are my own reasons why I continue to believe in God in the face of the agnosticism of our overly – adult world, and despite the dark nights that sometimes beset me.

First, I believe in God because I sense, at the deepest level of my being, that there's an unalienable moral structure to things.

Life, love, and meaning are morally contoured. There's an inalienable "law of karma" that's experienced everywhere and in everything: good behaviour is its own happiness, just as bad behaviour is its own sorrow.

Different religions word it differently but the concept is at the heart of all religion and is, in essence, the very definition of morality: "The measure you measure out will be the measure that's measured back to you." That's Jesus' version of it and it can be translated this way: "The air you breathe out is the air you will re-inhale."

Simply put: If we cut down too many trees we will soon be breathing in carbon monoxide. If we breathe out love, we will meet love. If we breathe out hate and anger, we will soon enough find ourselves surrounded by hatred and anger. Reality is so structured that goodness brings goodness and sin brings sin.

I believe in God because blind chaos could not have designed things this way, to be innately moral. Only an intelligent Goodness could have built reality this way.

My next reason for believing in God is the existence of soul, intelligence, love, altruism, and art. These could not have emerged simply from blind chaos, from billions and billions of cosmic bingo chips coming out of nothing, endlessly churning through billions of years.

Random chaos, empty of all intelligence, love, altruism, spirituality and art could not have eventually produced the soul and all that is inside it.

Can our own hearts and all that's noble and precious within them really be just the result of billions of fluke chances colliding within a brute, mindless process?

I believe in God because if our hearts are real, then so is God.

Next, I believe in God because the Gospel works- if we work it. What Jesus incarnated and taught ultimately resonates with what's most precious, most noble, and most meaningful inside life and inside each of us.

Moreover, this checks out in life. Whenever I have faith and courage to actually live out the Gospel, to roll the dice on its truth, it always proves to be true- the loaves multiply and feed the thousands and David defeats Goliath. But it doesn't work unless I risk it. The Gospel works, if we work it.

The objection could be raised here, of course, that many sincere, faith-filled people risk their lives and truth on the Gospel and, from all appearances, it doesn't work for them. They end up poor, as victims, on the losing side. But again, that's a judgment we make from the standards of this world, from the Gospel of Prosperity where, whoever has the most worldly success, wins.

The Gospel of Jesus undercuts this. Anyone who lives it out as faithfully as he or she is able will be blessed with something beyond worldly success – namely, the deeper joy of a life well-lived, a joy which Jesus assures us is deeper, less ephemeral, and more lasting than any other joy.

I believe in God because the Gospel works! As does prayer!

Finally, though certainly not least, I believe in God because the community of faith that stretches back to the beginning of time, that stretches back to the life and resurrection of Jesus, and that baptised me into the faith.

Throughout all of history, virtually all human communities have been also communities of faith, of belief in God, of worship, and of sacred ritual and sacrament.

I believe in God because of the existence of families of faith and the existence of Church and sacrament.

I wrote my doctoral thesis on the classical proofs for the exis-

tence of God, arguments for God's existence taken from some of the great intellectuals in history: Anselm, Thomas Aquinas, Descartes, Leibniz, Spinoza, and Alfred North Whitehead. I rambled through nearly 500 pages of articulating and evaluating these proofs and then ended up with this conclusion.

We don't come to believe in God because of the compelling power of some mathematical equation or logical syllogism. God's existence becomes real to us when we live an honest, sincere life.

My own urgent plea to the world out there is do not become part of the herd mentality as Albert Einstein so succinctly puts it from his short essay quoted in Chapter One, under "The Meaning of Life".

The Role of Family and Faith

But some things don't change for us humans as they are crucial in whatever era you live your life.

Fundamental things like family and faith and must always play an important role in your life.

That's the way God planned it

It is as simple as that.

Each of Us Has a Story to Tell

Each one of us has their own unique story to tell.

Each one of us has been given a conscience and a free will to choose how we want to live here on earth.

Each one of us has a journey to travel through life.

Each one of us must discern what the right way is and what the wrong way is.

Each one of us must make our own choices and then must live with the consequences.

This is where family and faith can play a critical role in creating abiding values and lay down sound principles to follow in order to lead a meaningful existence here on earth.

I Have Fought the Good Fight

It is my hope that you find the contents of this book helpful as you discern and make important decisions that in the final analysis you alone must make.

Surround yourself with caring family and friends and live out your faith. That way you surely have chosen the right path.

As for myself I like to believe that, in my own small way, I have practiced what I have preach – excuse the pun because as a deacon in my parish I preach a weekly homily on these very values, espoused in the sure belief that each one of us needs to constantly feed our human soul as we strive to do good in this world in the hope of sharing eternal rest in the presence of God in our next life.

These inspiring words from Timothy 4:7 are a constant reminder to me in my closing years and give me hope to continue to live and enjoy life to the fullest:

> *I have fought the good fight.*
> *I have finished the race.*
> *I have kept the faith.*

It is my fervent wish that you too can one day reflect positively on your journey in life.

Doug Boake

Husband, father, father-in-law, grandfather, friend, counsellor and deacon.

Bedfordview
2019

Chapter 1

I Believe

We live in a secular world where, in a religious sense, anything goes. The modern world demands that there be complete freedom of speech, thought and action.

Yet, each one of us experiences tension, struggle and fear every day.

Sadly God is forgotten.

In his book *Jesus Today - a Spirituality of Radical Freedom,* Albert Nolan, the famous South African Dominican theologian, responds to a widely felt need for a strong practical spirituality that is unmistakably relevant for the world today. He challenges us to think about the problems, crises and opportunities of our time. He says we must take Jesus seriously, as a mystic and a profound reader of the signs of his own times. Indeed, as Nolan contends, the spirituality Jesus lived by is more relevant today than ever. Ironically it is this serious engagement with both the modern world and Jesus' wisdom that leads us to a spirituality of joyful freedom as we develop a sense of oneness with God, with ourselves, with others and the entire universe.

In the Foreword of the book, Timothy Radcliffe OP explains that Nolan looks at the profound individualism that subverts our lives and happiness, as well as the effects of globalisation, for better or for worse. He says Albert also explores the silence and solitude, his meditation of God's forgiveness and, most beautifully, the role of women in his life. Resisting the looney imaginings of the *Da Vinci Code*, Albert shows us how deep Jesus' relationship with Mary Magdalene, the first patron of the Dominican Order, was and with Mary, his mother.

The first four chapters of the book give us a glimpse at the extremely complex and ever-shifting signs of our times. To say the least, one word says it all - startling - not only because we can now see that we are living on the edge of chaos, but also a giant leap forward in our history and our evolution seems to have become a reality. The penultimate chapter on becoming *One With the Universe* is especially stimulating, as Nolan points out that young people today are rarely interested in dogma and doctrine. This is so. And yet one can glimpse here the intimations of a new doctrine of creation that is not stuffy, that does not cramp our thoughts but liberates our imaginations, and as all good doctrine should, invites us to continue along the path of the mystery.

The signs of the time are pointers to the future. It is not that they show us clearly and definitively where we are going. Rather, the value of these pointers is that they challenge us. Or, to put it in terms of our faith, what matters is that we allow God to challenge us through our reading of the signs. What we have to avoid is the imposition of our pre-conceived ideas upon the reality of today. Our aim must be to face the truth about what is actually happening – whether we like it or not. Pointing fingers and finding people to blame for today's problems will simply blind us to the significance of the signs we are looking at.

He then analyses the challenges of our society and the spirituality of Jesus; he proposes a practical spirituality for today, one that offers a way forward for anyone, regardless of how busy or immersed in the daily affairs of our world he or she may be. In fact, one of the first challenges that we are offered is that of resisting the temptation of busyness, what Herbert McCabe called "the tyranny of work".

I thought it worthwhile to see what Albert Nolan wrote about *The Da Vinci Code*, a novel for adults, because it helps to explain the times in which we live in today:

Published early in 2004, Dan Brown's "The Da Vinci Code" has become the biggest selling novel in history. And the movie is set to break any number of box office records. What is it about our times that makes books and movies of this kind so extraordinarily popular?

"The Da Vinci Code" is a historical novel. However, it abounds in historical errors and displays considerable ignorance of the history of art and the structures of the Catholic Church. It has released an avalanche of criticism from academics, ecclesiastics, theolo-

gians, and especially historians which are fully dealt with in an article Da Vinci Fraud The Pastoral Review 1, no 5 *(2005): 71- 74 Gerald O'Collins. But this just seems to add to its appeal.*

In Dan Brown's novel, the great secret kept hidden for two thousand years, but handed down in a code known to only a few people, is that Jesus marries Mary Magdalene and they had a child called Sarah, and this royal bloodline continues down to this day. It makes for an intriguing storyline, especially in view of the present-day scholarly interest in the role of Mary Magdalene in the early Church. For a greater insight, you should read the article by Ed Conroy Resurrecting Mary Magdalene in National Catholic Reporter (July 15, 2005), 11-13.

The significance of "The Da Vinci Code" however, is not to be found in the accuracy or inaccuracy of its contents, but in the book's accuracy as a barometer of where we are today and what people are looking for. More and more people, and especially young people have given up all the certainties of the past: religious certainties, scientific certainties, cultural certainties, political certainties, and historical certainties. Everything is being questioned. They feel that one can no longer believe anything that authorities of any kind are saying and have been saying for centuries. Ours is an age of unprecedented scepticism. One opinion is as good as another. All one can say is that some opinions are old and boring, while others are interesting.

Academics call this attitude of mind post-modernism, and the popularity of "The Da Vinci Code" is a barometer or measure of just how widespread this way of thinking is. It is a sign of our times.

With this prevailing position in the world all around us, I feel it necessary to spell out in this book my own beliefs and thinking to explain where I personally stand in our modern, complex and fast-changing world.

Hopefully, in the process you too will find some answers to your doubts and be inspired to walk in faith in your journey to find expression to your own innermost feelings, unanswered questions and, in doing so honestly and with conviction, find peace and contentment.

I have found more inner peace in the later years of my life having finally surrendered to the will of God. It is so easy, yet it has taken me a lifetime to do it.

Gospel of the New Covenant

Dr Scott Hahn, one of the foremost theologians in the world, in his lectures to his students at the Franciscan University of Steubenville in Ohio, captures in a nutshell wonderfully what I believe and what I try to pass on others in my missionary obligation as a practicing Catholic.

He writes:

So let me attempt to sum up the Gospel of the New Covenant, starting at the beginning and going to the end, in ten basic steps.

First, we start with the good news of creation: God is more than a wise creator, he is also our loving Father. That is why he made us "in his own image, to live as his children, by his grace. He is not far from any of us, and he gives us the power to live, to move, and to be who we are. We are his children" (Acts: 27 -28).

Second, God established a covenant with us from the beginning. A covenant is a sacred family bond in which persons give themselves to one another in loving communion. God calls us into a covenant to share friendship with him and each other as his family. To keep his covenant, we must trust and obey our Father in everything, just as we love each other as his sons and daughters. "Have we not all one father? Has not one God created us? Why then are we faithless to one another, profaning the covenant of our fathers?" (Malachi 2:10. Christian Evangelical Version Bible - CEV).

Third, all of us have broken God's covenant. That's what sin is about. More than broken laws, broken homes and broken hearts. We see it all around us: in society, at work and at home. We're selfish, dishonest, mean and miserable. "They are proud, conceited and boastful, always thinking up new ways to do evil…… They know God has said who acts this way deserves to die. But they keep doing evil things, and they even encourage others to do them" (Romans 1:29-32, CEV). That's why the Father punishes sin with death - because sin kills the life of God within us and others.

Fourth, we desperately need God's mercy and grace. We'd like to think there is a simpler solution – more education, laws, technology or money. But that's like prescribing aspirins for AIDS! Sin's infection is too deep and deadly. But we shouldn't despair or get depressed. Our Father knows what we need better than we do. "Once we were also ruled by the selfish desires of our bodies and minds. We had made God angry, and we are going to be punished.

But God was merciful! We were dead because of our sins, but God loved us so much that he made us alive with Christ" (Ephesians 2:3-4).

Fifth, the solution to our sin came when God became man in Jesus Christ. Jesus took on our weak and mortally wounded nature, not only to heal and perfect us but to elevate us to share in his own life of divine sonship, to make us one with his father. "Jesus and the people he makes holy all belong to the same Family. That is why he's not ashamed to call them his brothers and sisters" (Hebrews 2:11). Jesus did what no else could do: he took sin away at its source. "We are people of flesh and blood. That is why Jesus became one of us. He died to destroy the devil, who has power over death. But he also dies to rescue all of us who live each day in fear of dying" (Hebrews 2:14-15). Through his suffering and death, we are healed and brought home. This gives us the greatest confidence and hope. "See what love the Father has given us, that we should be called children of God; and so we are" (1 John 3:1, CEV).

Sixth, Jesus seals the New Covenant with us through his self-offering. This sacrifice began in the Upper Room, at the Passover meal, when he said to his disciples: "Take, eat; this is my body"... And he took a cup, and he gave it to them, saying; "Drink of it, all of you; for this is my blood of the covenant, which is poured out for many for the forgiveness of sins" (Matthew 26:26-28, CEV). Christ sacrificed himself for us, first by instituting the Eucharist, and then by dying for us on Calvary. It is all one piece.

Seventh, Jesus was raised from the dead by the power of the Holy Spirit. And the Holy Spirit is his gift to us. "Now that we are his children, God has sent the Spirit of his Son into our hearts. And his Spirit tells us that God is our Father" (Galatians 4:6). God promises to give the Spirit to all who ask: "As bad as you are, you still know how to give good gifts to your children. But your heavenly Father is even more ready to give the Holy Spirit to anyone who asks" (Luke 11:13).

Eighth, the Holy Spirit comes to us through the sacraments in a powerful way; for Jesus instituted them, and now administers them to us, beginning with baptism. "Now the name of our Lord Jesus Christ and the power of God's Spirit have washed you and made you holy and acceptable to God" (1 Corinthians 6:11). The greatest of the seven sacraments is the Eucharist. It is the sacrifice of the New Covenant and the family meal that nourishes us with Jesus' own body and blood, just as he promised: "I am the bread of life....My flesh is true food, and my blood is the true drink. If you eat my flesh and drink my blood, you are one with me and I am one with you" (John 6:48, 55-56). Now he calls us to share this living Bread at the Father's table. "Listen! I am standing and knocking at your door. If you hear my voice and open the door, I will come in and we will eat together" (Revelation 3:20).

Ninth, the Catholic Church is God's worldwide family that the Father sent the Son to establish by the Spirit. "Just as I am one with you and you one with me, I also want them to be one with us" (John 17:21). So we love the Church as our Mother, revere it as Christ's bride and obey its teachings, all because we trust Jesus will be true to his word: "On this rock I will build my Church, and death itself will not have any power over it"(Matthew 16:18). But Jesus doesn't stop there; he also gives us his mother, Mary, to be our own spiritual mother. "When Jesus saw his mother and the disciple whom he loved standing there, Jesus said to his mother, 'Woman, there is your son'. Then he said to the disciple, 'There is your mother' (John 19:26-27, see Revelation 12:1-2, 5 and 17). Mary's grace all comes from Jesus. That's what makes her so powerful in God's family. No one ever honoured his mother like Jesus; he now wants us to imitate him.

Tenth, as God's children, we are earthly pilgrims heading home to heaven. This makes heaven our true homeland, and death a true homecoming! "We are citizens of heaven and are eagerly awaiting for our Saviour to come.....and make these poor bodies of ours like his glorious body" (Philippians 3:20-21). And the angels and saints who have gone before us are our older brothers and sisters". You have now come to Mount Zion and the heavenly Jerusalem.

This is the city of the living God where thousands and thousands of angels have come to celebrate. Here you will find all of God's dearest children.....And you will find God himself".

(Hebrews 12:22-23).

If there is one thing that sets the Catholic Church apart from all other religions, it is the understanding of the Eucharist as the real body and blood of Jesus consecrated at every Mass.

No easy matter to expect young people in their Catechism classes to have understood this adequately, although explained to them by very dedicated Catechism teachers who generously share their faith and time.

But the foundation of real faith should be taught in the home again no easy matter for busy parents.

Faith is Caught, Not Taught

A wise old quotation, often repeated by our parish priest Fr Tony Kelly many years ago, struck a chord with me when he said: *Faith is caught, not taught.*

In other words parents have the responsibility of creating the right atmosphere at home where faith is practiced so children can learn by example. Sadly many practicing parents and devout Catholics themselves did not have the Eucharist properly explained to them or failed to understand fully this wonderful sacrament or really ever believed in this important mystery of their faith.

With faith you will still experience doubt and fear from time to time.

Understanding the Eucharist

I read an interesting article by my favourite Catholic columnist, Fr Ronheiser, who wrote a beautiful and simple real life story to explain the primal understanding of the Eucharist:

Christian is de Cherge, the Trappist Abbott who was murdered in Algeria in 1996, tells this story of his First Communion. He grew up in a Roman Catholic family in France and on the day of his First Communion he said to his mother: "I don't understand what I'm doing".

She replied simply: "It's OK, you don't have to understand it now, later you will understand."

Jesus, no doubt, must have given his disciples the exact same advice at the Last Supper, at their First Communion, when he offered them bread and said, "This is my body", and then offered them wine and said, "This is my blood". They would not have understood. There would have been considerable confusion and bewilderment. How are we supposed to understand this? What does it mean to eat someone's body and drink someone's blood? I suspect that in the face of their non-understanding, like Christian de Cherge's mother, Jesus would have also said:" You don't have to understand it now, later you will understand".

Jesus didn't give a theological discourse on the Eucharist at the Last Supper. He simply gave us a ritual and asked us to celebrate it regularly, irrespective of our intellectual understanding of it. One of his more explicit explanations of the meaning of the Eucharist was his symbolic action of washing his disciples' feet.

Little has changed. We too aren't asked to fully or even adequately understand the Eucharist. Our faith only asks that we are faithful in participating in it. In fact, as is the case for all deep mysteries, there is no satisfactory, rational explanation of the Eucharist. Nobody, not a single theologian in the world, can, to anyone's satisfaction, adequately lay out the phenomenology, psychology, or even spirituality of eating someone else's body and drinking his blood. How is this to be understood? The mind comes up short. We need instead to rely upon metaphors and icons and inchoate, intuitive understanding. We can truly know this mystery, even if we can't fully understand it.

During my seminary and academic training, I took three major courses on the Eucharist. After all those lectures and books on the Eucharist, I concluded that I didn't understand the Eucharist and that I was happy enough with that because what those courses did teach me was how important it is that I celebrate and participate in the Eucharist. For all the intellectuality in those courses, their true value was that they ultimately said to me what Christian de Cherge's mother said to him on the day of his First Communion: "You don't have to understand now, later you will understand." Contained in that, of course, is the fact that there is something profound here that is worth understanding, but that it's too deep to fully grasp right now".

Perhaps, this can be helpful in our search for what to say to some of our children and young people who no longer go to church and who tell us that the reason they don't go is that they don't find the Eucharist meaningful. We hear that lament all the time today: "Why should I go to church; it doesn't mean anything to me?" That objection is simply another way of saying what young Christian de Cherge said to his mother at his First Communion: "I don't understand this". Perhaps our answer then could be along the lines of the response of his mother: "You don't have to understand now, later you will understand".

The British theologian, Ronald Knox, had this to say about the Eucharist:

We have never, as Christians, been truly faithful to Jesus, no matter our denomination. In the end, none of us truly followed those teachings which most characterise Jesus: We haven't turned the other cheek. We haven't forgiven our enemies. We haven't purified our thoughts. We haven't kept our hearts pure and free of the things of this world. But we have been faithful in one very important way: we have kept the Eucharist going. The last thing Jesus asked us to do before he died was to keep celebrating the Eucharist.

And that we've done. But we've been faithful in doing it because we grasped the wisdom in what Christian de Cherge's mother said to her son.

Meaning of Life

I was encouraged by the philosophy of Albert Einstein when I came across his short essay *The World as I See It* on the meaning of life, in particular, the need we all have for a little of mysticism:

How strange is the lot of us mortals? Each of us is here for a brief sojourn; for what purpose he knows not, though he sometimes thinks he senses it. But without deeper reflections, one knows from daily life that one exists for other people - first of all for those on whose smiles and wellbeing our own happiness is wholly dependent, and then for the many, unknown to us, to whose destinies we are bound by ties of sympathy. A hundred times a day I remind myself my inner and outer life are based on the labours of other men, living and dead, and that I must exert myself in order to give in the same measures I have received and am still receiving...

I have never looked upon these with ease and happiness as ends in themselves – this critical basis I call the ideal of a pigsty. The ideals that have lighted my way and time and have given me new courage to face life cheerfully, have been Kindness, Beauty and Truth. Without the sense of kinship with men of a like mind, without the occupation with an objective world, the eternally un-

attainable in the field of art and scientific endeavours, life would seem empty to me. The trite objects of human efforts – possessions, outward success and luxury – have always seemed to me contemptible.

My passionate sense of social justice and social responsibility has always contrasted oddly with my pronounced lack of the need for direct contact with other human beings and human communities. I am truly a "lone traveler" and have never belonged to my country, my home, my friends, or even my immediate family, with my whole heart; in the face of all these ties, I have never lost a sense of distance and a need for solitude.

My political ideal is democracy. Let every man be respected as an individual and no man idolised. It is an irony of fate that I myself have been the recipient of excessive admiration and reverence from my fellow-being, through no fault and no merit of my own. The cause of this may well be the desire, unattainable for many, to understand the few ideas to which I have with my feeble powers attained through ceaseless struggle. I am quite aware that for any organisation to reach its goals, one man must do the thinking and directing and generally bear the responsibility. But the led must not be coerced, they must be able to choose their leader. In my opinion, an automatic system of coercion soon degenerates; force attracts men of low morality. The really valuable thing in the pageant of human life seems to me not the political state, but the creative, sentient individual, the personality; it alone creates the noble and the sublime, while the herd as such remains dull in thought and dull in feeling.

The most beautiful experience we can have is the mysterious. It is a fundamental emotion that stands at the cradle of true art and true science. Whoever does not know it and can no longer wonder, no longer marvel, is as good as dead, as his eyes are dimmed.

It was the experience of mystery- even if mixed with fear- that engendered religion. A knowledge of the existence of something we cannot penetrate, our perception of the profound reason and the most radiant beauty, which in their most primitive forms are accessible to our minds, constitutes true religiosity. In this sense, and in this sense only, I am a deeply religious man. I am satisfied with the mystery of life eternal and with a knowledge, a sense of the marvellous structure of existence, as well as a humble attempt to understand even a tiny portion of the Reason that manifests itself in nature.

The Seven Sacraments

It was only -recently, at a meeting of Rite of Christian Initiation for Adults that our parish priest, Fr Laszlo Karpati, who grew up in Hungary under Communist rule, surprised the group when he asked which was the most important sacrament.

The group considered the seven sacraments in turn: Baptism, Confirmation, Eucharist, Matrimony, Reconciliation, Holy Orders and Anointing the Sick, and tried to decide which was the most important. He surprised us by saying that over the years he had come to realise that life itself was the most important sacrament. This seems to me to reinforce what Einstein thought about the meaning of life.

The liturgical life of the Catholic Church revolves around the Eucharistic sacrifice and the sacraments. The purpose of the sacraments is to make people holy, to build up the body of Christ, and finally, to give worship to God; but being signs, they also have a teaching function. They not only pre-suppose faith, but by words and objects, they also nourish, strengthen, and express it; that is why they are called "sacraments of faith". The sacraments impart grace, but, in addition, the very act of celebrating them pre-disposes the faithful to receive this grace in a fruitful manner, to worship God with due reverence and to practice charity.

Worship is integral to our lives as Christians. When we engage in the prayer and ritual of the Church, we are formed as Church. Our sacramental rites are of primary importance while we are gathered.

So there are two fundamental ideas which constantly recur in the Church's teaching on the sacraments.

First, there is the Church's concern for these instituted by Christ, their number and their proper preservation and administration; then the grace which Christ has for all time linked to these signs and which is communicated by them.

The second is the effect of the sacraments. They are the signs of Christ's work; the effectiveness of Christ's continuing work in his Church cannot be dependent on man's inadequacy. A sacrament, administered properly in the way established by Christ and with the proper intention, gives the grace it offers. It is effective not by reason of the power of intercession of priestly prayer nor on account of the worthiness of the recipient, but solely by the power of Christ. The power of Christ lives in the sacraments. The effect of the sacrament is independent of the sinfulness or unworthiness of the minister.

St Leo the Great said: *Whatever was visible in Our Redeemer has passed over into the Sacraments.*

Here is a wonderful way of explaining the sacraments by Michael Francis Pennock in his book *This is Our Faith.*

What is more valuable than love? Love is precious, but it is also fragile. When we've had a bad day, when people misjudge us, when tragedy strikes or setbacks come our way, we are tempted to forget that we are loved. At such times we need to be reminded. A smile, a humorous card, a hug, a sympathetic word – these symbols of love remind us that we are special, loved and cared for.

We need symbols because we are body-people. We need concrete signs to express mysteries like love. We need to say and to hear loving words, to give and receive gifts, to kiss and be kissed, to shake hands, to write and receive notes of appreciation. This is true in our relationship with other people; it is also true in our relationship with God.

The seven sacraments – Baptism, Confirmation, Eucharist, Reconciliation, Healing, Matrimony and Holy Orders – are symbols of God's love, signs of His grace. Sacraments and sacramental life are absolutely central to Catholic identity and belief. To reflect on their meaning and to appreciate what they represent – God's presence to us in our ordinary life – is to grow in an understanding of what Catholics hold to be very precious. In a real sense, the sacraments are the embodiment of the good news of God's love.

The Apostles' Creed

We can get terribly bogged down and hot under the collar with history, especially as far as religion is concerned. It is said that more wars have been fought in the name of religion than for any other reason.

The history of the origin of the Apostles' Creed is a point in question. The Apostles' Creed proclaims the great and wonderful deeds which God has done for us. It is a profession of our faith for which the Apostles died and which was handed down to us through the centuries.

It was the Church community that kept the Apostles' Creed as a great treasure, protecting it from being changed and mutilated by wrong teachings.

> *I believe in God, the Father almighty,*
> *Creator of heaven and earth.*
> *I believe in Jesus Christ, his only son, our Lord.*
> *He was conceived by the power of the Holy Spirit*
> *and born of the Virgin Mary.*
> *He suffered under Pontius Pilate,*
> *was crucified, died and was buried.*
> *He descended to the dead.*
> *On the third day He rose again.*
> *He ascended into heaven,*
> *and is seated at the right hand of the Father.*
> *He will come again to judge the living and the dead.*
> *I believe in the Holy Spirit,*
> *the holy Catholic Church,*
> *the communion of saints,*
> *the forgiveness of sins.*
> *the resurrection of the body,*
> *and life everlasting*
> *Amen.*

Although it has its roots in apostolic times, embodies apostolic teaching and had an important place in the early church, The Apostles' Creed, as legend has it, took shape at the dictation of the Twelve Apostles, each of whom contributed a special article. Thus, Peter, it is alleged, under the inspiration of the Holy Spirit, commenced: *I believe in God the Father Almighty;* Andrew (according to others) continued: *And in Jesus Christ, His only Son, Our Lord.* James the Elder went on: *who was conceived by the Holy Spirit etc.* I nevertheless like to believe parts of the legend are true, as who better to write the Apostles' Creed than the Twelve Apostles themselves!

However according to Rev James Dodd in his book *Exposition of the Apostles Creed*:

The real origin of the Creed has now been traced with great exactness. The original germ of it is to be sought for in the baptismal confession made by converts in the reception of that rite. The primitive confession may have contained no more than "I believe that Jesus Christ is the Son of God," but we have evidence within the New Testament itself that it soon became enlarged. Paul speaks of the "form of teaching" delivered to converts (Romans 6:17), and reminds Timothy of "the good (beautiful) confession" he had made in the sight of many witnesses (1 Timothy 6:12). Similar language is used of Christ's confession before Pilate (1 Timothy 6:13). We may perhaps conjecture from the Epistles that Timothy's confession contained references to God as the author of life, to Jesus Christ and His descent from David, to His witness before Pontius Pilate, to His being raised from the dead, to His coming again to judge the living and the dead (1 Timothy 6:13; 2 Timothy 2:8; 4:1). Early Christian writers, such as Ignatius (110 AD) and Aristides the apologist (circa 125 AD), showed traces of other clauses.

In its Trinitarian Form, the Apostles' Creed, it is perceived, has no theological or metaphysical character. It is not only the oldest, but the simplest and least developed of all creeds. It is a simple enumeration, in order, of the great verities which the Church was known to have held, and to have handed down from the beginning - which Scripture also taught. Originating from the baptismal confession, it naturally follows the Trinitarian order suggested by the customary formula for baptism. The first article in the Creed declares belief in God the Father Almighty, Maker of heaven and earth. The second to the seventh articles declare belief in Jesus Christ, His only Son, our Lord, and in the great facts embraced in the Gospel testimony regarding Him. The eighth article affirms belief in the Holy Spirit to which the additional clauses, declaring belief in the holy Catholic Church, the communion of saints, the forgiveness of sins, the resurrection of the flesh (body), and the life everlasting were added.

Mary Mother of God

After Mary gave her famous consent to becoming the Mother of God:*"Behold the handmaid of the Lord; let it be done to me according to thy word"* (*Luke 1 38-39*), she goes with haste to help her cousin Elizabeth, who is delighted to see her. Our Lady then expresses her joy in the Magnificat, one of the most beautiful verses in the Bible (*Luke 1 46-55*):

> *My soul magnifies the Lord*
> *and my spirit rejoices in God my Saviour;*
> *Because He has regarded the lowliness of His handmaid;*
> *For behold, henceforth all generations shall call me blessed;*
> *Because He who is mighty has done great things for me,*
> *and holy is His name;*
> *And His mercy is from generation to generation*
> *on those who fear him.*
> *He has shown might with his arm,*
> *He has scattered the proud in the conceit of their heart.*
> *He has put down the mighty from their thrones,*
> *and has exalted the lowly.*
> *He has filled the hungry with good things,*
> *and the rich He has sent away empty.*
> *He has given help to Israel, his servant, mindful of his mercy* even
> *as he spoke to our fathers, to Abraham and his posterity forever.*

Clearly Mary, in hastening to help her cousin, is focused on service to others. In this way, she glorifies the Lord in reflecting (and "magnifying") His goodness and love. And, of course, by becoming the Mother of God she will help Him redeem us for our salvation in His Passion.

Speaking of magnifying, Archbishop Fulton J Sheen once referred to our Blessed Mother as being like *a magnifying glass that intensifies our love of her Son.*

Note that Mary's joyful claim that '*all generations shall call me blessed*' in no way takes away her humility. If she seems to boast here, it is much as St Paul does later on in 2 Corinthians 10:17 when he says '*whoever boasts, should boast of the Lord*', that is to say, in God's work being done through us.

In this regard, the Magnificat is more than a prayer of praise. It also reminds us of the essential link between humility and holiness. Just as God has regarded the holiness of His handmaid and has done great things for Mary in making her the Mother of His Son, so too *"He has put down the mighty from their thrones (with His own might) and has exalted the lowly."*

How about you? Does your soul magnify the Lord? We may never be able to approach Him from Mary's level of sanctity as the Mother of God. Still, we are all called to be saints.

As St Ambrose once said in referring to this wonderful prayer: *"Let Mary's soul be in us to glorify the Lord; let her spirit be in us as we rejoice in God our Saviour."*

Another major point of division between the Catholic and other Christian Churches is the role of Mary, mother of Jesus. She is highly venerated in the Catholic Church for humbly accepting the invitation to be the mother of Jesus as part of God's ultimate plan for the salvation of the human race. Mary is highly exalted and a dominate focus of adoration and devotion and for intercessory prayers of the faithful.

According to eyewitnesses, the Virgin Mary has appeared to a number of people over the centuries in many parts of the world, the more notable visitations are Lourdes in France, Fatima in Portugal, Guadalupe in Mexico, Medjugorje in Bosnia-Herzegovina and Knock in Ireland. These apparitions on earth are thoroughly investigated by the Church to establish the authenticity of the sightings before giving them the Church's blessings as places of worship.

The remarkable story of Knock in Ireland, the Apparition, which was witnessed in 1879, is further proof of the presence of Mary in our lives. On 21st August 1879, at approximately eight o'clock in the evening, 15 people from the village of Knock in County Mayo witnessed an Apparition of Our Lady, St Joseph, St John the Evangelist, a Lamb and cross on an altar on the gable wall of the Parish Church. The witnesses watched the Apparition in the pouring rain for two hours, reciting the Rosary. Although they themselves were saturated, not a single drop of rain fell on the gable or vision. There were 15 official witnesses to the Apparition, most of whom were from the village of Knock and surrounding areas and ranged from just five years old to 74 years old. Each of the witnesses gave testimonies to a Commission of Enquiry in October 1879. The findings of the Commission were that the testimonies were both trustworthy and satisfactory.

Lourdes

Another well-documented appearance of Mary was on the evening of 11th February 1858. A young Roman Catholic girl, Bernadette, went to fetch some firewood with her sister and another child when a Lady, who was indescribably beautiful, appeared to her at the Massabielle Grotto in Lourdes in France. Although the Lady did not tell Bernadette her name when asked at first, she told her to go to the grotto. On subsequent visits, the Lady revealed herself to be the Immaculate Conception.

This was a reference to the dogma of the Immaculate Conception which had been defined only four years earlier in 1854 by Pope Pius IX, stating that the Virgin Mary had been conceived without sin.

Bernadette, having only a rudimentary knowledge of the Catholic faith, did not understand what this meant but she reported it to her parish priest. He, initially very sceptical of Bernadette's claim, became convinced when he heard this because he knew the young girl had no knowledge of the doctrine. The Lady also told Bernadette to dig in the ground at a certain spot and to drink from the small spring of water that began to bubble up. Almost immediately cures were reported from drinking the water. And yet the water has been shown through repeated testing not to have any special curative properties.

Today thousands of gallons of water gush from the source of the spring, and pilgrims are able to bathe in it. Countless purported miracle cures have been documented there, from the healing of nervous disorders and cancers to cases of paralysis and even blindness.

During the Apparitions, Bernadette Soubirous prayed the Rosary.

Pope Saint John Paul ll wrote: *The Rosary of the Virgin Mary is a prayer with great significance to bring fruits of holiness.*

Lourdes is not just about a story of a poor peasant girl, the wondrous things she experienced, and the town she lived in.

The story and subsequent events are just one of many ways in which God's message is conveyed to the world. In this case, a message of Healing and Hope.

The experience of Lourdes may reveal that message and the healing, or conversion process by God's grace, gets underway. God's healing is there for all. We do not even have to wait for Jesus to say *stretch out your hand (Luke 6:10),* we just have to offer it, to be healed.

Underlying all this is the ultimate message of Hope. Our Lady did not promise to make Bernadette happy in this world, nor us, as we struggle to faithfully follow the Way. In this context *we are the people who have been through a great trial* but the promise, as of that to Bernadette, is that our happiness will be in the other, *where we will never hunger and thirst again; sun and scorching will never plague us, because the Lamb who is at the heart of the throne will be our shepherd and will guide us to springs of living water; and God will wipe away all tears from our eyes (Revelation 7:16, 17).*

I visited Lourdes in September 2017 to attend a Deacon's conference on *"Salvation and Healing in a Diaconal Church".* The first keynote address was by Cardinal Luis Antonio Tagle from the Philippines, from a Catholic perspective, followed by a presentation by Dr Kjell Nordstrokke from an Evangelical Lutheran perspective and Dr Etienne Grieu SJ on the perspective in France. It was interesting to hear the different issues facing the Church in various countries of the world.

But it soon became clear to me that the issues the Church faces in Africa are very different and more challenging, as the Catholic Church in Africa is relatively young, more missionary in outlook and has to reconcile with cultural and tradition issues but nevertheless is growing rapidly in numbers. However, the substantial resources received from overseas in the past in the form of financial aid and handouts, as well as missionary priests, brothers and sisters from the many congregations like the Comboni Missionaries of the Heart of Jesus, the Missionaries of Africa (the White Fathers), Society of Jesus (Jesuits), to name but a few, are drying up. Therefore the building of new churches and establishing, or even just continuing existing Catholic schools, the lifeblood of the Church, combined with a lack of governmental aid, needs urgent attention and innovative ways are needed to address these issues. Each community will in the future have to become a more self-sufficient, caring community, called upon to make greater self-sacrifices in order to provide churches, schools and religious for the faithful.

For me personally, it was gratifying to see the increasingly important role deacons are playing in the affairs of the living Church all over the world at the conference. Seeing the different projects undertaken by deacons was inspiring, from the establishment of temporary refugees facilities in Africa and Europe, to feeding schemes and many other simple but effective projects to improve the lives of their communities. However, problems such as those experienced by homeless in those communities have no easy solutions.

Politicians have failed to provide solutions, so it is up to communities themselves to address this growing problem. The key thing is just to make people comfortable and then work from there. Initially, these people must be given the basics – warm clothing, some hot food, a decent bed - then they can start to cope, and a little more then becomes possible: work opportunities, permanent homes and addressing their own particular needs.

It was also a pleasure to meet Bishop First from Germany who assisted greatly with funds for the establishment of St Augustine College, a Catholic University established in Johannesburg, largely due to the untiring efforts of Sister Edith Raidt from the Schoenstatt Order.

The miracle of Lourdes for me was meeting with Renzo Battani whom I had known in Johannesburg for 50 years as a client. He was clearly searching for some direction in life after a close family member had recently been murdered and his brother Mario had died: he had retired from work, sold his home and had cycled from Lisbon to Fatima and then to Santiago where, on the second day on his stay, his bicycle was stolen with all his worldly possessions. It was an unforgettable experience when we came across each other in an open field and took a selfie as a memento of our chance meeting. As I listened to his sad story I realised that there was a real need for Hope and Faith in our lives, and places like Lourdes and Fatima help with the individual situations in which we find ourselves from time to time.

Reconciliation

The Sacrament of Penance and Reconciliation (commonly called confession) is one of the seven Sacraments of the Catholic Church and is one from which the faithful obtain absolution for the sins committed against God and neighbour and are reconciled with the community of the Church.

By this sacrament, Christians are freed from sins committed after baptism. The Sacrament of Penance is considered the normal way to be absolved from mortal sin, by which one would otherwise condemn oneself to separation from God after death. As Scriptural basis for this sacrament, the Catechism of the Catholic Church No 1443 states:

The words 'bind' and 'loose' mean whomever you exclude from your communion, will be excluded from communion with God; whomever you receive anew into your communion, God will welcome back.

This Catholic practice is much misunderstood and criticised by many who possibly don't know where this important sacrament came from and, more importantly, the need for and benefit of reconciliation in our daily lives.

In John 20:23 Jesus told his disciples before dying on the cross:

Whose sins you forgive, they shall be forgiven.

Whose sins you retain, they shall be retained.

This is a great consolation to an individual. Knowing the wrongs we have committed in our life from time to time are unconditionally forgiven by a priest on the direct instruction of Jesus so we are able to pick up the threads of life again and not be burdened by the weight of our sins. Sure, there are T's and C's to be complied with in order to obtain a proper absolution for our sins- this is to be expected. However these are not onerous, but spiritual peace is absolutely necessary in order to continue living our Christian life.

God is the only One able to forgive our sins as he is an ever-loving God who genuinely understands the fragility of our human nature.

The real point of this Sacrament is that a person must first be prepared to admit to themselves that what they have done is wrong, secondly to be prepared to change their sinful ways, thirdly to genuinely be sorry and finally, to ask for forgiveness from God.

Chapter 2
Prayer

The great Archbishop Oscar Romero, martyred 38 years ago, had a lovely response to people who offered prayers when faced with a problem: *To pray and then sit back and wait for something to happen, isn't holiness – it's laziness.*

So having started to contemplate to pray what happens next is important.

Some action is needed from ourselves. We cannot possibly be reminding God something He already knows, God knows that already. Nor can we be trying to change God's mind – it is a definitive characteristic of God that God is unchanging.

Raymond Perrier, writing in his column *Faith and Society* titled a recent article in the Southern Cross: *What Do We Pray For?* He offered the following thought-provoking explanation for ordinary people like you and me of the power of prayer and asked us what we feel the act of prayer in itself is actually doing. This was at the time when Catholics and people of many other faiths were praying for rains to come to avert the water crisis which engulfed Cape Town.

Theologians have grappled for centuries to try to the purpose of prayer. I am unlikely to solve that in a few hundred words. But one explanation I do find convincing is that prayer is effective not because it changes the heart of God but because it changes our hearts. As soon as we pray for something, we automatically become more aware of it.

So taking the example of the water crisis in Cape Town we may be moved to take action to campaign for more efficient management or more equal distribution of water, or for speedier response to leaking pipes; or for action to halt the climate change that is disrupting our weather patterns. All of these can be effective even if not immediately.

But there is also something, I can do which is immediate. But that takes effort. I could wait till the threat of my own Day Zero before I sort out leaking taps; take shorter showers; turn off the water when I brush my teeth or stop washing my car with drinking water. And I could hope that last-minute prayers will then make up for my years of complacency and wastefulness. Or I could take action now. It will require some behavioural adjustments.

So let's keep praying for rain. And let's pray that the act of praying will change our hearts and our behaviour so that each one of us reduces the amount of water we use, shares what we have more fairly with others, and takes much more interest in what we do about climate change.

That is the kind of miracle that is worth praying for.

We might feel that we are already grateful for our food, but formally saying Grace before a meal, especially if said loud and with other people, makes sure that we really are grateful and we remember those who are without food.

Simple Prayer

Most Christians shy away from praying because of misconceptions and fears they have about prayer. So the obvious question to ask must be: What is prayer?

St Augustine says prayer is you simply talking to God.

No flair. No technicalities. No special formulas.

Just talking and making time to listen to God in our daily lives.

Here is a simple prayer which comes straight from the heart.

> *Dear God,*
> *I need you.*
> *Every day, every moment, every second that I breathe,*
> *I need you.*
> *I am not strong enough on my own.*
> *Amen.*

But we anguish over many questions we ponder on deeply before we truly understand the relationship God wants with us:

How can I possibly talk to God?

Does God know who I am?

What do I say to him?

Will God really listen to me?

It is hard to recognise that God is present when our lives seem to be crashing down around us. When our days are dark with despair there is always hope knowing that He is waiting for us to invite Him. Just as we wait in hope for the Resurrection, we remember that no matter how dark our days may be, there is always Hope.

Here is a prayer you can say:

> *Lord give me the strength during the days*
> *when I am filled with despair to know*
> *there is always Hope with you.*
> *Amen.*

In today's difficult conditions, the needs of so many people are very real and pressing but sadly many people no longer know how to pray to find answers to their needs.

The traditional forms of prayer, particular of personal prayer, are regarded as so out of date that one no longer dare mention them to the faithful, who can speak freely only about communal prayer. Yet the forms this prayer takes have, for many people, turned the green pasture of Christian prayer into a desert.

Now if there is one sphere in which warmth and spontaneity must never be stifled it is certainly in that of personal prayer, for this prayer is the expression of life and our holy relationship to God. This relationship must declare itself in our lives, for each fibre our being is linked to God.

Our prayer must embrace every kind of human activity. It is a constant and many-blossomed flowering, springing from our being children of God.

Fr Ron Rolheiser OMI wrote a recent article "Our Critical Need To Pray". In it he said:

The late Fr Daniel Berrigan wrote: "Unless you somehow have a foot outside your culture, the culture will swallow you whole."

Fr Berrigan's profound statement is true too in this sense: Unless you can drink in strength from a source outside yourself, your natural proclivities for paranoia, bitterness, and hatred will invariably swallow you whole. The disciples in Luke's Gospel under-

stood this. They approached Jesus and asked him to teach them how to pray because they saw him doing things that they did not see anyone else doing.

He was able to meet hatred with love, to genuinely forgive others, to endure misunderstanding without giving in to self-pity and bitterness, and to retain within himself a centre of peace and non-violence.

This, they knew, was as extraordinary as walking on water, and they sensed that He was drawing the strength to do this from a source outside Him, through prayer.

They knew they themselves were incapable of resisting bitterness and hatred, and they wanted to be as strong as Jesus. So they ask him: 'Lord, teach us to pray'.

And so, we have the greatest prayer of all.

It must undoubtedly be the prayer Jesus gave to His disciples on His way to His death on the cross. The disciples implored Jesus to remember them when He came to His kingdom and teach them how to pray.

First Jesus told them, according to Matthew 6:5, how not to pray:

And when you pray, do not be like the hypocrites, for they love to pray standing in the synagogues and on the street corners to be seen by others. Truly I tell you, they have received their reward in full. But when you pray, go into your inner room, shut your door, and pray to your Father, who is unseen. And your Father who sees what is done in secret will reward you.

Jesus told his disciples about the parable of the Pharisee and Tax Collector according to Luke 18:9 to warn them when they prayed about making comparisons with others and who were confident of their own righteousness and looked down on everyone else:

Two men went up to the temple to pray, one a Pharisee and the other a tax collector. The Pharisee stood by himself and prayed: "God, I thank you that I am not like other people – robbers, evildoers, and adulterers – even like this tax collector. I fast twice a week and gives a tenth of all I get".

But the tax collector stood at a distance. He would not even look up to heaven, but beat his breast and said, "God, have mercy on me, a sinner".

I tell you that this man, rather than the other, went home justified before God. For all those who exalt themselves will be humbled, and those who humble themselves will be exalted.

According to Matthew 6:9-13 and Luke 11:2-4 Jesus then told them how are to pray.

Our Father

> *Our Father who art in heaven,*
> *hallowed be your name; Your kingdom come;*
> *Your will be done*
> *on earth as it is in heaven.*
> *Give us this day our daily bread;*
> *and forgive us our trespasses,*
> *as we forgive those who trespass against us;*
> *and lead us not into temptation,*
> *but deliver us from evil.*
> *Amen.*

The Catechism of the Catholic Church teaches that the Lord's Prayer (also called the Our Father or Pater Noster) is truly the summary of the Gospel.

The disciples of Jesus were familiar with the concept of praying, but they still asked Jesus to teach them how to pray. They knew that they should pray and they really wanted to do it the right way.

We know that Jesus prayed regularly and He expects us to pray daily as well. From his teachings we get an idea what he expects from us.

In Matthew 6:5-8 we read the well-known *Sermon on the Mount* in which Jesus was very explicit how we should go about praying, which, unfortunately, seemed to have been largely ignored by many faiths, even more so by social media, world leaders and politicians.

And, when you pray, do not use vain repetitions as the heathen do. For they think that they will be heard for their many words. Therefore do not be like them. For your Father knows the things you have need before you ask Him.

Jesus begins by addressing His Father in heaven. So we too begin our personal prayers in like manner, in doing so we also recognise the deep relationship God desires to have with us – we who are called and who respond to God's calling can rightfully be children of God.

In their bestselling book *Journey of the Spirit* which is equally loved by Catholics and Protestants, the joint authors Trevor Hudson and Morton Kelsey write this about what must be the most well-known prayer in the world:

Our Father, who art in heaven

Throughout his life on earth Jesus spoke directly to God in Aramaic, addressing him 'Abba', meaning 'my own dear father'. Never before had anyone dared to pray as intimately like this. Imagine the astonishment of the disciples when they were invited to pray as Jesus did. They were being offered the privilege of coming to God in the same way that Jesus did.

When we call God 'Abba, Father', the image that immediately comes to mind is the father in Jesus' parable of the prodigal son. So it will be helpful when we begin praying to see ourselves as prodigals returning home, having messed up our lives in various ways. We can imagine the Father there with open arms and gifts that go beyond our wildest imaginings. Here is God accepting us as we are, assuring us of our belonging and welcoming us home. When we hold this picture before us, we realise that there is nothing we cannot talk about with God. We can be totally open, transparent and honest.

When we recite the "Our Father", we should say the words slowly so we can focus on the meaning of each phrase. The ideal would be we should say this prayer every day so we be able to judge how each of our daily actions compare with God's expectation for us and, more importantly, what needs our attention in future to prevent repeating our shortcoming.

Hallowed be your Name

So to begin, to 'hallow' God's sacred name and hold it in the highest regard and with very deep respect, we may have blasphemed by swearing, using God's name in vain or being disrespectful.

This is a common bad habit easily eliminated if we became aware of it and conscientiously try to amend our ways.

Many of the Psalms show examples of how to praise and honour God.

Your kingdom come

We have the promise that God's Kingdom will soon be established on earth and that it will be ever-expanding. It is easy to see that only the Kingdom of God will give this world the true peace and security we yearn for.

Your will be done on earth as it is in heaven

In Matthew 7:21 Jesus says "Not everyone who says to Me, 'Lord, Lord' shall enter the kingdom of heaven, but he who does the will of My Father in Heaven." We should, therefore, endeavour to learn what God's will is and strive earnestly to bring our own will into harmony with His will. This we do by reading the Bible quietly and regularly by ourselves, in addition, and better still by being part of a weekly bible study group and attending specific courses to discuss what is meant by the particular readings. This helps us to get to know Him as He feeds us with spiritual food.

Give us this day our daily bread

This reminds us that we need to ask and thank God for food, drink and other physical things, but also ask Him for spiritual food to feed our souls on a daily basis.

That's why grace is important for families at mealtimes as we pray:

And forgive us our trespasses, as we forgive those who trespass against us *(Matthew 6:14).*

We all sin daily and we need to ask daily for forgiveness. This is very hard for most of us to forgive others for what they have done to us. But, if we don't forgive and forget the sins that we think others have committed against us, we have no chance of being forgiven ourselves.

Jesus was very emphatic about this: "For if you forgive men their trespasses, your heavenly Father will also forgive you. But if you do not forgive men their trespasses, neither will your Father forgive your trespasses" (Matthew 6:15).

And do not lead us into temptation, but deliver us from the evil.

Satan the devil is the accuser of the brethren (Revelation 12:10) and the evil one. He is very clever, abounds in subtlety and hates those who love God. He will never give up in his vicious attempts to separate us from our heavenly Father through temptation and sin.

But the all-powerful God can deliver us if we seek His help and draw close to Him (James 4:7-8).

After His resurrection, Jesus spoke with His disciples for 40 days. They asked Him during that time if He was going to restore the Kingdom then *(Acts 1:6).*

One of the things Jesus will do on His return to earth is to establish the Kingdom for God, and all the other kingdoms will be no more (*1 Cor 15:24*). What a glorious event that will be!

Amen.

The Gospels, almost all the Epistles (James and 3 John are the exceptions) and the book of Revelations all close with Amen.

This word is also one of the names referring to Jesus: And to the angel of the church of the Laodiceans write, 'These things says the Amen, the Faithful and True Witness, the Beginning of the creation of God *(Revelation 3:14).*

Saying Amen also means we agree that what went before is true.

Jesus indicated in Matthew 6 that we should begin our prayers by addressing our heavenly Father and close them with Amen.

We also have the incredible privilege to add "In Jesus's Name" before we close *(John 14:13-14).*

Family Grace

Meals are an important time to realise how lucky we are to have enough to eat and give God thanks.

Here are three blessings, although there are hundreds of prayer forms that can be used before meals:

> *O Lord,*
> *Bless this food we are about to receive,*
> *and the hands which prepare it*
> *and keep us ever mindful of the needs of others.*
> *In Jesus' name, Amen.*

Here is a grace especially suitable for younger children which is very easy to teach:

> *Thank you for the food we eat,*
> *Thank you for the world so sweet,*
> *Thank you for the birds that sing,*
> *Thank you, God for everything. Amen.*

This clever grace, even a little amusing, by Robert Burns, the famous Scottish poet.

> *Some Folk hae meat that canna eat,*
> *And some can eat that want it;*
> *But we hae meat, and we can eat,*
> *So let the Lord be Thanket! Amen.*

Mealtime is undoubtedly the best opportunity for the family to witness and play out their faith in front of each other. To me it is indeed encouraging, gratifying and humbly to listen as members of the family, including young children, take turns to spontaneously express their appreciation to God and relate back to the day's experiences and events.

Family mealtimes are generally the only time the family can get together and enjoy themselves in each other's company. There should be a special time set aside for the evening meal in the home at which cell phones, I-Pads, computer games and television are not allowed.

This physical expression of faith by the family at evening meals will always be looked back on with fond memories as family ties are strengthened.

Our former parish priest, Mngr Tony Kelly, constantly reminded us of this important habit in family life with the oft-repeated message '*Families that pray together, stay together*'.

Be prepared for stares from strangers in restaurants and from your guests at family celebrations. Most times I believe they secretly admire this display of faith, and who knows, they too may feel comfortable adopting this wonderful visible display of thanksgiving for daily blessings in their own lives.

The real tangible benefits of sitting around a table for a family meal are emphasised by Father Larry Richards, a well-known priest in the USA, who conducts retreats, delivers lectures countrywide and appears on radio and TV programmes. He says that in today's world it is absolutely vital for families to communicate with each other and share daily experiences and, by so doing assisting each other with issues and challenges as a family unit.

He offers a few practical examples adopted by his family when the children were growing up in an unhappy home, where his Irish father was an alcoholic policeman and his mother had to struggle to keep the family together. Although it was not practical for the family to share a meal together every night, one rule of their home was that nobody should eat alone. So a family member was expected to sit and converse with that family member who would otherwise have eaten alone because school, work or sport made them late for the family evening meal.

Another absolute rule of his family was that every member of the family was expected to attend a family meal over the weekend, usually Sunday lunch when their Italian mother went to great lengths to prepare a huge spread which took hours to consume. He says that these times were not necessarily happy family reunions as there was invariably infighting and family squabbles. But he makes the point that the family got together and aired their grievances and unhappiness and shared good experiences with each other, which helped clear the air and cemented their relationships anew. Years later, these family meals together were fondly remembered for particular episodes and created happy memories.

Prayers to the Saints

We humans need role models to guide and inspire us during our time on earth, as the high point of humanity is written by the lives of people of conscience, especially those who paid the ultimate price for being true to their conscience. Conscience is that mysterious inner capacity of every human being to distinguish right from wrong and choose to act accordingly.

Who could fail to be inspired and influenced by the thousands of men and women who made the supreme sacrifice of martyrdom?

My own two favourite saints for their statements of faith are John the Baptist who, pointing to Jesus, said '*He must increase, and I must decrease*', and St Thomas More who opposed King Henry the Eighth's marriage to Anne Boleyn and was beheaded. His final words were "*The King's good servant but God's first.*"

He also inspires me, as he said that just because something is lawful does not mean it is morally right.

The practice of being named a saint has been practiced by Catholic and Orthodox Churches for many centuries. To be called a saint generally means that a dead person must be credited with having performed two miracles.

Since miracles are considered proof that the person is in heaven and can intercede for us, the miracle must take place after the candidate's death and as a result of a specific petition to the candidate. The practice of praying to saints is based on the idea that they are now in heaven listening to those prayers.

Three-quarters of Christians belong to Churches that pray to dead saints for intercession. In Africa, it is customary to pray to the ancestors who are always consulted and are venerated as part of the different cultures.

The followers of Christ – the saints – obey His instructions and prayed to the Father. They worshipped God only.

The Bible records a time when the Apostle John came into the presence of a powerful spiritual being, and even though he was in awe and fell down before the being, he was quickly reminded to venerate and worship God only. *"Then he said to me, 'See that you do not do that. For I am your fellow servant, and of your brethren the prophets, and of those who keep the words of this book. Worship God.'" (Revelation 22:9).*

Prayers to Mary, Mother of God

> *Hail Mary, full of grace,*
> *the Lord is with thee;*
> *blessed art thou among women,*
> *and blessed is the fruit of thy womb, Jesus.*
> *Holy Mary,*
> *Mother of God,*
> *pray for us sinners,*
> *now and at the hour of our death. Amen.*

This prayer, called the Hail Mary and taken from Luke 1:28, is recited daily by millions of Roman Catholics around the world. It is part of a larger sequence of devotions called the Rosary, which derives its name from a Latin word meaning a wreath or garland of roses. It is also commonly called the Ave Maria and forms the basis of the Angelus prayer recited by devotees throughout the world who paused in what they were doing three times a day.

We pay special honour to the Blessed Virgin because she is

the Mother of God, and our Mother. God has exalted her above all other creatures. Her intercession is more powerful with God than that of any other saint. No man refuses his mother a favour; so God does not refuse any request of Mary.

The eighth and final chapter of Lumen Gentium which was issued by Vatican Council II on 21 November 1964 as one of its principal documents, is about the Blessed Virgin Mary, Mother *of* God in the Mystery of Christ and the Church, and explains the understanding of the role of Mary in the Church:

Mary's function as mother of men in no way obscures or diminishes the unique mediation of Christ, but rather shows its power. But the Blessed Virgin's salutary influence on men originates not in any inner necessity but in the disposition of God. It flows forth from the the merits of Christ, rests on his mediation, depends entirely on it and draws all its power from it. It does not hinder in any way the immediate union of the faithful with Christ but, on the contrary, fosters it.

The predestination of the Blessed Virgin as Mother of God was associated with the incarnation of the divine Word: In the designs of Divine Providence she was the gracious mother of the divine Redeemer here on earth, and above all others and in a singular way the generous associate and humble handmaid of the Lord. She conceived, brought forth, and nourished Christ, she presented Him to the Father in the temple, shared her Son's sufferings as He died on the cross. Thus, in a wholly singular way she co-operated by her obedience, faith, hope and burning charity in the work of the Saviour, in restoring supernatural life to souls. For this reason, she is a mother to us in the order of grace.

This motherhood of Mary in the order of grace continues uninterruptedly from the consent which she loyally gave at the Annunciation and which she sustained without wavering beneath the cross, until the eternal fulfillment of all the elect. Taken up to heaven she did not lay aside this saving office but by her manifold intercession, she continues to bring to us the gifts of eternal salvation.

By her maternal charity, she cares for the brethren of her Son, who still journey on earth surrounded by dangers and difficulties, until they are led into their blessed home. Therefore the Blessed Virgin is invoked in the Church under the titles of Advocate, Help-

er, Benefactress, and Mediatrix. This, however, is so understood that it neither takes away anything from nor adds anything to the dignity and efficacy of Christ, the one Mediator.

Essentially, we believe that Mary's body was taken to heaven before she experienced physical death (the Assumption) where she was crowned and exalted as Queen of Heaven and continues to function as the Mother of God in heaven.

In 1950 Pope Pius X11 declared ex cathedra (meaning it is considered infallible) that The Immaculate Mother of God, the ever-Virgin Mary, having completed the course of her earthly life, was assumed body and soul into heavenly glory.

The Rosary

In his book *Being Catholic* Mitch Finley recognises that being Catholic today means being a seeker, a pilgrim, and a person with questions, doubts and insecurities.

He writes:

One of the most popular forms of Catholic devotional prayer is the Rosary. For many centuries, through constant social and cultural change, Catholics have retained a special affection for the Rosary. Something about the repetitive nature of the prayers and the simplicity of the mysteries that go with each set of ten Hail Marys touches the Catholic heart.

The Rosary is a physical form of prayer, and being embodied spirits we appreciate a form of prayer that gives us something to hang onto. The beads of a Rosary slip through our fingers as we pray, and that can be a comfort.

The educated reader who wants a more in-depth understanding of the Rosary would do well to consult one of the more articulate recent works published on the subject. In his excellent book A Western Way of Meditation, The Rosary Revisited David Bryan says that the Rosary is 'clearly the world's most popular form of meditation'.

Stations of the Cross

During the six weeks of Lent culminating on Good Friday, Catholics the world over traditionally practice the devotion of the Stations of the Cross, although the devotion is not limited to Lent.

We prayerfully recall the last stage of the journey that Jesus walked in his earthly life: from his death sentence by Pontius Pilate until he was taken to Golgotha, to be crucified and buried in a garden nearby, in a new tomb hewn out of the rock.

This devotion, known as *"The Way of the Cross"* and in the Holy Land as *"The Via Dolorosa"*, has evolved over time. In fact, after the Roman Emperor Constantine legalised Christianity in the year 313, this pathway was marked with its important stations.

There are 14 traditional stations:

First station	**:Pilate condemnation of Christ todeath**
Second station	**: Jesus carries the cross**
Third station	**: Jesus falls the first time**
Fourth station	**: Jesus meets his Blessed Mother**
Fifth station	**: Simon of Cyrene helps carry the cross**
Sixth station	**: Veronica wipes the face of Jesus**
Seventh station	**: Jesus falls the second time**
Eighth station	**: Jesus consoles the women of Jerusalem**
Ninth station	**: Jesus falls the third time**
Tenth station	**: Jesus is stripped of his garments**
Eleventh station	**: Jesus is nailed to the cross**
Twelfth station	**: Jesus dies on the cross**
Thirteenth station	**: Jesus is taken down from the cross**
Fourteenth station	**: Jesus is laid in the tomb**

Some modern liturgists say that the traditional Stations of the Cross are incomplete without the final scene, the fifteenth station depicting the empty tomb and/or the resurrection of Jesus, because Jesus' rising from the dead was an integral part of his saving work on earth.

The object of the Stations of the Cross is to help the faithful to make a spiritual pilgrimage of prayer through meditating upon the chief scenes of Christ's suffering and death. A plenary indulgence is granted to the faithful who make the pious exercise of the Way of the Cross.

However, nothing more is required of the faithful than a pious meditation on the passion and death of the Lord, which need not be a particular consideration of the individual mysteries of the stations.

During Lent, as the deacon in our parish, I begin the Stations of the Cross with this story written in 1923 by Dr James Alan Francis to set the scene as we reflect on how Jesus has had more impact on mankind than any other person.

One Solitary Life

He was born in an obscure village
the child of a peasant woman.
He grew up in another obscure village
where he worked in a carpenter shop
until he was thirty when public opinion turned against him.
He never wrote a book.
He never held an office.
He never went to college.
He never visited a big city.
He never travelled more than two hundred miles
from the place where he was born.
He did none of the things usually associated with greatness.
He had no credentials but himself.
He was only thirty three.
His friends ran away.
One of them denied him.
He was turned over to his enemies
and went through the mockery of a trial.
He was nailed to a cross between two thieves.
Whilst dying, his executioners gambled for his clothing,
the only property he had on earth.
When he was dead,
He was laid in a borrowed grave
through the pity of a friend.
Twenty centuries have come and gone and
today Jesus is the central figure of the human race
and the leader of mankind's progress.
All the armies that have ever marched.
All the navies that ever have ever sailed.
All the parliaments that have ever sat.
All the kings that ever reigned put together
have not affected the life of mankind on earth
as powerfully as that
One Solitary Life.

Statues

Many a Catholic has been accused of praying to statues, which is simply not true.

This misconception is further perpetuated by the magnificent and priceless paintings and statues of Jesus, Mary and the saints to be found in churches ranging from the Vatican to the most humble of churches in remote villages in many parts of the world.

The question is posed in *Rome Sweet Home* by Scott and Kimberley Hahn:

Why are these allowed and even encouraged by the Catholic Church when one of the Ten Commandments condemns the making of graven images and bowing down before them?

According to the Old Testament whilst Moses was given the Ten Commandments by God on Mount Sinai, the people below had grown tired of waiting for Moses to come down the mountain so they made a golden calf to worship. This was pure idolatry and condemned by Moses so much so that in his fury at seeing this, he hurled the two tablets of the Ten Commandments onto the ground, smashing them to pieces.

However, we read in the Bible that the Israelites were given specific instructions for images to be made as part of the Holy of Holies – garden imagery and the cherubim over the mercy seat for example.

God even commanded Moses, as we read from the Book of Numbers 21:9, to make a bronze serpent on a pole, which the people were to look upon in order to be healed from the bites.

To bring this to the world we live in today, we all hang pictures of the family up in our homes or carry the photos of loved ones in our wallets or can access photos on our cell phone, iPad or on our computers. What do these do for us? The obvious answer is that they remind us of people close to us – spouse, children, parents, deceased relatives or friends.

Either God got his commands mixed up, or the point of the command is not to worship the images.

That's what the paintings and statues do – they remind us of these wonderful religious people who play an important role in our everyday life. We love them and thank God for them.

It seems strange that during the sacred time of the year we cover everything that is beautiful in our churches, even the crucifix. Shouldn't we be looking at the painful scene at Calvary while we listen to the Passion narratives on Palm Sunday? And why go through such lengths to cover images that are designed to raise our hearts and minds to heaven?

First of all, we use veils to alert us to the special time of Lent. When we walk into the church and notice everything is covered with purple cloth, we immediately know that something is different. The last two weeks of Lent are meant to be a time of immediate preparation for the Sacred Triduum and these veils are a forceful reminder to get ready.

Secondly, the veils focus our attention on the words being said at Mass. When we listen to the Passion narrative, our senses are allowed to focus on the striking words from the Gospel and truly enter into the scene.

Thirdly, the church uses veils to produce a heightened sense of anticipation for Easter Sunday.

And therein lies the whole point: the veils are not there forever. The images need to be unveiled; it is unnatural for them to be covered.

The unveiling before the Easter Vigil is a great reminder of our own life on earth. We live in a "veiled" world, in exile from our true home. It is only through our own death that the veil is lifted and we finally able to see the beauty of everything in our lives.

Intercessory Prayer

God appreciates people who pray fervently for other people facing trials. Jesus in the midst of His greatest trial prayed not only for Himself but for His disciples and for us:

As You sent Me into the world, I also have sent them into the world. And for their sakes I sanctify Myself, that they may be sanctified by the truth (Luke 22:42).

I do not pray for these alone, but also for those who will believe in Me through their word; that they may be one, as You, Father, are in Me, and I in You; that they also may be one in Us, that the world may believe that You sent Me (John 17: 18-21).

Jesus did not just focus inward, but His words and His prayers showed that He wanted love and joy and peace and patience and all the fruit of God's Spirit for His followers (*John 13:17*).

God gives us instructions to pray for others in several places in the Bible:

- The Apostle James tells us to *'pray for one another, that you may be healed'* (*James 5:16*).
- The apostle Paul encourages us to intercede for Church members and ministers: *'praying always with all prayer and supplication in the Spirit, being watchful to this end with all perseverance and supplication for all the saints- and for me, that utterance may be given to me, that I may open my mouth boldly to make known the mystery of the gospel, for which I am an ambassador in chains'* (*Ephesians 6:18-20*).
- Jesus even commanded *'Love your enemies, bless those who curse you, do good to those who hate you, and pray for those who use you and persecute you'* (*Matthew 5:44*).

Why does God want us to pray for others? Because intercessory prayer reflects God's own character of outgoing love and mercy. God wants us to think as He does, and praying for others helps us to think beyond ourselves and to grow in compassion for others.

Eucharistic Adoration

Part of a person's prayerful life is to spend time in the presence of the Lord. This is when you take time out from all your daily activities and worries to listen in silence to what God wants you to hear. Otherwise, our minds are so busy that we simply shut God out so He is not part of our life. With time and practice, this becomes a much appreciated time to be valued in our journey of life.

At the end of our Chemin de Compostella in October 2017, we visited the beautiful cathedral of Sacre-Coeur in Paris, where I found this quotation in a framed picture at the entrance – it was written by Pope Benedict XVI on why Eucharistic adoration should be part of our lives:

Eucharistic adoration is an essential way of being with the Lord......

In the sacred Host, Jesus is present.......

Only by adoring His presence do we learn to receive Him properly – we learn the reality of communion, we learn the Eucharistic celebration from the inside.

Let us love being with the Lord.

There we can speak with Him about everything. We can offer Him our petitions, our concerns, our troubles, our joys, our gratitude, our disappointments, our needs and our aspirations.

Therefore we should also constantly pray for the harvest Jesus commanded us. The harvest is plentiful, but the workers are few. Ask the Lord of the harvest, therefore, to send out workers into his harvest field' (Matthew 9:37-38)

Jesus commanded us to pray for the harvest. The harvest is ripe and is now. Do not postpone to tomorrow what you can do today. All it takes for evil to abound is for good men to do nothing. So our efforts to spread the good news must be seen.

Mass

Mass is boring. I don't get anything out of Mass so why should I go? Why can't I pray alone? Many adults and, more so, young people express these feelings to justify why they no longer attend Mass, so I will try and explain briefly the reasons why I personally attend daily Mass.

The great American Bishop Fulton J Sheen, the process for whose canonisation for sainthood has begun, who was known for his dynamic preaching and especially his work on television and radio, once gave a talk on the meaning of Mass at a retreat for teenagers.

He said: *'If you don't get anything out of Mass, it's because you don't bring the right expectations to it. The Mass is not entertainment. It is worship of the God who made us and saves us. If we have a correct understanding of Mass, it will become more meaningful for us. We will want to go to Mass. We will understand why the Mass is God's precious gift to us, and we wouldn't think of refusing that gift.'*

James Stenson is an educational consultant specialising in family life and the family-school relationship. In his book *Life: The Religious Upbringing of Your Children* and other books, has this to say about the importance of Mass in your life:

"If you really thought about who you are, who God is, and how much thanks you owe Him, you would want to go to Mass. The Mass would become the source and centre of your spiritual life."

How should we respond to Jesus' final instruction to his disciples at the Last Supper: *"Do this in memory of me"*?

The Mass was instituted at the Last Supper by Jesus before his Crucifixion. The Last Supper was the first Mass.

According to Luke 22:14-20:

When the hour came, Jesus and his Apostles reclined at the table. And he said to them, 'I have eagerly desired to eat this Passover with you before I suffer. For I tell you, I will not eat it again until it finds fulfillment in the kingdom of God'.

After taking the cup, he gave thanks and said, 'Take this and divide it among you. For I tell you I will not drink again from the fruit of the vine until the kingdom of God comes.'

And he took bread, gave thanks and broke it, and gave it to them, saying, 'This is my body given for you; do this in remembrance of me.' In the same way, after supper he took the cup, saying, 'This cup is the new covenant in my blood, which is poured out for you.'"

When we celebrate the Mass, we repeat the Last Supper, as Jesus commanded us to do. In doing this, we remember and re-present his great love for us on the Cross – taking our sins upon himself so that we, if we follow his commandments, can live with him forever after death.

The Catholic Church was established by Jesus himself. We read in the Gospel (*Matthew 16:18-19*) that Jesus made Peter the head of his Church- the first Pope - when he said: *"I say this to you, you are Peter, and upon this rock I will build my Church and the gates of hell shall not prevail against it. I will give you the keys to the kingdom of heaven. Whatever you bind on earth shall bound in heaven, and whatever you loose on earth will be loosed in heaven."*

The Church teaches that we must fulfill the command of Jesus by attending Sunday Mass or the Vigil Mass the night before - Saturday evening - to fulfill our obligations.

The Catechism of the Catholic Church (*1994, pg 493-494*) explains that Mass attendance on Sundays and Holy Days of Obligation is the first of six commandments of the Church.

These Commandments of the Church also require receiving Communion at least once a year during the Easter season, confessing any mortal sin as a preparation for Communion, and observing the prescribed days of fasting and abstinence. These Commandments spell out the minimal responsibilities of a Catholic. To fail to fulfill them through our own fault is a serious sin in the eyes of the Church.

We should obey the teachings of the Church - as we saw above Jesus made Peter the head of his Church and gave Peter and the Church the keys to the kingdom of heaven.

The Church's authority in faith and morals is absolute because Christ's authority is absolute.

So to answer the question 'what do we do at Mass?', it is necessary to explain what the Mass is all about in easy language in order to get a correct and proper understanding so that the Mass becomes more meaningful for us.

Firstly, the Mass is a sacrifice – a perfect sacrifice, created by Jesus himself. Through the priest, we offer Jesus, Body and Blood, to the Father, just as Jesus offered Himself to the Father on the Cross. In an unbloody way, we repeat, make present, Christ's death and Resurrection. Through this memorial of Jesus, we offer God our praise, sorrow for our sins and deepest thanks.

Secondly, the Mass is also a meal because at the Consecration the bread and wine, through the power of the Holy Spirit, become the real Body and Blood of Christ. We Catholics believe that this is not merely symbolic, but it is the real flesh and real blood of our Lord Jesus, under the appearance of bread and wine. This is known as the transubstantiation – the conversion of the substance of the Eucharistic elements into the Body and Blood of Christ at consecration - only the appearances of bread and wine still remaining.

When we receive Holy Communion, we receive Jesus Himself. He is real food for our soul.

Jesus said this very plainly in John 6:55-56: *"I say this to you, unless you eat the flesh of the Son of Man and drink his blood, you do not have life within you. Whoever eats my flesh and drinks my blood has eternal life, and I will raise him on the last day. My flesh is true food, and my blood is true drink. Whoever eats my flesh and drinks my blood remains in me and I in him."*

One Saturday morning at Mass at the Schoenstatt Shrine in Bedfordview Father Mariano Perez of the Comboni Fathers asked us a simple question during his homily: *Why do you come to church every Sunday?* He then explained why we, in fact, should attend Mass week in and week out. He suggested that it was not because we had a religious obligation to attend Mass to fulfill our responsibilities as Catholics.

The real answer must be because it strengthens our union with Jesus; He lives within us in a special way. It cleanses us from venial sins whilst serious sins called mortal sins require forgiveness in the Sacrament of Reconciliation (confession).

It gives us the grace to avoid sin in the future. It increases our love of God and neighbour.

We worship with other people, as God wants us to come together in community to worship Him. Jesus said in Matthew 18:20: *'Where two or three are gathered together in my name, there am I.'*

We need to give God a chance to give us grace and strength by attending Mass and receiving Holy Communion. If we bring an attitude of devout prayer and thanksgiving to Mass, God will pour out on us great spiritual riches: consolation, confidence, peace, deep happiness and spiritual strength for the challenges of life.

Mother Teresa once wrote: *'Jesus is my God. Jesus is my Spouse. Jesus is my Life. Jesus is my everything. Because of this, I am never afraid.'*

Mother Teresa went to Mass every day. If we love the Mass as she did, we too will live in Jesus and He in us, and we will never be afraid.

I have attended Mass every day for the past 20 years or so. Many years ago I attended an early morning Mass on a Holy Day of Obligation at Christ the King Cathedral in Saratoga Avenue in Doornfontein. There were only five of us at Mass. To my absolute surprise, Mother Teresa walked in front of me to receive Communion at the altar. I will forever cling to the memory of her being small in stature, very devout in her prayers during Mass and very humble as she received the Body of our Lord. No great fuss as she simply did what was important in her saintly life. It made a lasting impression on me.

It was therefore especially to be important to me, when we faced 10 years of criminal and civil proceedings with the Scorpions and the law, to attend daily Mass for spiritual strength and inner peace, as the odds were heavily stacked against us until we were finally cleared of criminal charges on Friday 13th December 2013.

During this time I went further in my journey of faith when I was ordained a Deacon in the Catholic Church on 30th April 2011.

Here is a true and moving story passed on to me by Sr Marie Claire of Schoenstatt Sisters of Mary, from the lips of the late Father Stanislavsky SS.CC as related to Sister M Veronica Murphy:

One day many years ago, in a little town in Luxembourg, a captain of the Forest Guards was in deep conversation with the butcher when an elderly woman entered the shop.

The butcher broke off the conversation to ask the old woman what she wanted. She had come to beg for a little meat but had no money. The captain was amused at the conversation which ensued between the poor woman and the butcher.

"Only a little meat, but how much are you going to give me?"

"I am sorry I have no money, but I'll hear Mass for you."

Both the butcher and the captain were good men but very indifferent about religion, so they at once began to scoff at the old woman's answer.

"All right then," said the butcher. "You go and hear Mass for me and when you come back, I'll give you as much meat as the Mass is worth."

The woman left the shop and returned later. She approached the counter and the butcher seeing her said, "All right, we'll see'" He took a piece of paper and wrote on it, "I heard a Mass for you'" He then placed the paper on the balance scales and a tiny bone on the other side but nothing happened. Next, he placed a piece of meat instead of the bone on the scale, but the paper proved heavier. Both men were beginning to feel ashamed of their mockery and their game. Next a large piece of meat was placed on the scales but still, the paper held its own.

The butcher, exasperated, examined the scales but found they were all right. "What do you want, my good woman, must I give you a whole leg of mutton?"

At this, he placed a leg of mutton on the scale but the paper outweighed the meat. A larger piece of meat was put on, but again the weight remained on the side of the paper. This so impressed the butcher that he was converted and promised to give the woman a daily ration of meat.

As for the captain, he left the shop a changed man, an ardent lover of daily Mass. Two of his sons became priests, one a Jesuit and the other a Father of the Sacred Heart.

Father Stanislaus finished by saying, "I am the Religious of the Sacred Heart and the captain was my father."

From the incident, the captain became a daily Mass goer and his children were trained to follow his example. Later when his sons became priests, he advised them to say Mass well every day and never miss the Sacrifice of the Mass through any fault of their own.

Chapter 3
Faith

Catholicism

To understand my faith you need to know that I am a practicing Catholic - serving in the parish of St Joseph in Primrose, South Africa, as a deacon since 30th April 2011.

Lynne, my wife, is a sacristan in the parish and together we are involved in presenting the programme of RCIA (Rite of Christian Initiation for Adults) for those who seek a deeper understanding of the Catholic Faith and for preparing adult participants who wish to be baptised for the first time and be confirmed in the church.

I preach a homily at one of the Masses each weekend – a 9-minute homily which usually takes 4 to 5 hours each week to research, prepare and is constantly tweaked during the week as I turn over in my mind if I am are conveying the right message about the weekend readings. I am very conscious of the fact that for many people attending weekly Mass is the only time that they hear the Word of God. So this time for the homily is very important to impart, to inspire, and to explain the readings and teachings of God.

On Wednesday 7th February 2018, Pope Francis spoke on a topic close to home for me and the people in the pews, offering his recipe for what makes a good homily, saying they should be short and well-prepared, and the people also have to make an effort to listen and be patient with the limitations of their pastor.

The Pope said:

Those listening have their part to do. Mass-goers must give the appropriate attention, thus assuming the proper interior dispositions, without subjective demands, knowing that every preacher has both his merits and his limits.

Sometimes there's a reason to get annoyed about an overly long homily, one that lacks focus or that's incomprehensible, or at other times, it's actually the prejudice of the listener which creates obstacles. Whoever gives the homily must be conscious that they are not doing their own thing, they are preaching, giving voice to Jesus. Because of this, homilies must be well prepared, and they must be brief – no more than 10 minutes!

To drive the point home, Francis told a story, recounting how a priest had once told him that when visiting another town where the priest's parents lived, a father had confided in him: I'm happy because my friends and I found a church where they do Mass without a homily.

"How many times have we seen people sleeping during a homily, or chatting among themselves, or outside smoking a cigarette?" he said. *When people laughed at the notion, Francis responded, saying: "It's true, you all know it..... it's true!"*

Pope Francis urged those giving a homily, whether it's a priest, deacon or bishop, to remember that they are offering a real service to all those who participate in Mass.

The homily has been a source of pastoral concern and interest for the Pope since the beginning. He devoted a large portion of his 2013 *Apostolic Exhortation on Evangelic Discourse* to this subject as he explains his thoughts: *"But it is rather a way of resuming that dialogue which has already been opened between the Lord and his people, so it finds fulfillment in life."*

On the readings, he noted that while all the readings are significant, the Gospel is especially important, which is seen by the fact that the priest kisses the text and incenses it before reading the daily passage, and the congregation stands to listen to the reading of the Gospel.

Pope Francis said: *"From these signs, the assembly recognises the presence of Christ who brings them the Good News which converts and transforms."*

The pope explained further that the congregation doesn't stand to hear the Gospel itself, but Christ, who speaks to us through the reading:

"It is for this reason that we are attentive, because it's a direct conversation. The Word of Jesus which is in the Gospel is living and arrives in my heart. And because Jesus still communicates

with us through the Gospel readings at every Mass, we must give our response in our lives."

It is a fact that our own religious beliefs are either because of what our parents followed, the particular circumstances we find ourselves in either at the school we attended or the spouse we married, or because we made a conscious decision to join a particular faith for whatever reason.

I owe my faith to my mother who, having lost her mother at the tender age of 4, attended the Belgravia Convent in Johannesburg run by caring and dedicated Dominican Sisters who shaped her life and religion. The five Boake boys were placed in Osney House for boarders at the Pietersburg English Medium Primary School and were baptised and confirmed in their teens in the Pietersburg Catholic Cathedral. I owe a huge debt of gratitude to the Dominican Sisters at the Pietersburg Convent who persevered with very reluctant little boys with religious instructions after Mass on Sundays. Certainly, the breakfast at the end of each lesson helped us to stay the course of instruction in the faith!

My father was an Anglican in name only but, in his defence, he grew up and worked on the family farm called *Papkuil*, then served in North Africa during World War II. Later his building trade took him to remote areas all over the Lowveld and Bechuanaland Protectorate. I recall a few Christmases when he allowed himself to accompany the family to Mass largely because my sister Maeve implored him to make the effort. In his own way, he worked out his religion in a practical manner, rather than being religious. So when he died at the age of 68 from heart failure during his sleep, I was very relieved to find a Bible opened on his bedside table at John 3:16: *"For God loved the world so much that he gave his only Son, so that everyone who believes in him, may not die but have eternal life."*

This is the memory I treasure of my father as it gave me much comfort when I looked back at his role as a good father.

Lynne lost her father at the age of eight and owed her faith to her mother. The family of three girls, Lynne, Sue and Diane, lived in relative poverty, as their mother had to go out to work to earn a living. The girls were schooled in a Catholic convent at reduced fees and this grounding gave them a firm foundation and family security in growing up.

As there are many serious misunderstandings and misconceptions as to why one-third of the world's population practice Catholicism, I would like to explain a little about the Catholic Faith.

Here are some definitions as written by Michael Francis Pennock in his book *This is My Faith*.

- A Catholic is a Christian who belongs to a certain faith community that shares Jesus' vision and responds to his presence in our midst.
- A Catholic loves each member of their community and uses his and her unique talents to contribute to it in a positive way.
- A Catholic believes in God, who is our loving Father. This loving Father has made us brothers and sisters to everyone who has ever loved. Moreover, he has sent us His Son Jesus Christ who won for us our salvation and gave us eternal life.
- A Catholic believes in the presence of the Holy Spirit, accepting and using the many gifts he showers on us. By the power of this Holy Spirit, a Catholic accepts Jesus into his or her life.
- A Catholic attempts to live in harmony with Jesus' teaching: loving God above all things; loving neighbour as oneself; forgiving enemies; extending special care to the poor, lonely and outcast.
- A Catholic prays and lives a sacramental life, for example, the need for forgiveness through the celebration of the sacrament of reconciliation. Moreover, a Catholic cherishes the Eucharist as a special sign of God's nourishing love, a way to encounter the living Lord Jesus.
- A Catholic participates fully in the Eucharistic celebration every week.
- A Catholic reveres and reads the Bible, the Word of God.
- A Catholic acknowledges the role of the proper authority in the Church by seeking guidance for moral decisions from the Church's official teachers, the Pope and the bishops in communion with him.
- A Catholic serves others and shares his or her faith in public by acknowledging Jesus Christ and who is willing to stand

up to ridicule and suffering in the service of the gospel truth (*Romans 3,28 Galatians 2,16*).

- A Catholic is all of the above and more, including the distinguishing trait in his fierce stand and works for the preservation of human life.

The Code of Canon Law of the Catholic Church (Introduction by Pope John Paul II - New Revised English Translation dated 25th January 1983) is part of the distant heritage of law contained in the books of the Old and New Testaments. It is from this, as from its first source that the whole juridical and legislative tradition of the Church derives. For Christ the Lord in no way abolished the bountiful heritage of the law and the prophets which grew little by little from the history and experience of the People of God in the Old Testament. Rather He fulfilled it (*Matthew 5, 17*) so that it could, in a new and more sublime way, lead to the heritage of the New Testament.

Accordingly, although St Paul in expounding the mystery of salvation teaches that justification is not obtained through the works of the law but through faith (*Gal 2:16*), nonetheless he does not exclude the binding force of the Decalogue (*Roman 13:8-12; Gal 5, 13-25:6*) nor does he deny the importance of discipline in the Church (*1 Cor 5, 6*). Thus the writings of the New Testament allow us to perceive more clearly the greater importance and to understand better the bonds which link it ever more closely with the salvific character of the Gospel message.

It is instructive for practicing Catholics to read the Code of Canon Law:

No 748 (1): *All are bound to seek the truth in the matters which concern God and his Church; when they have found it, then by divine law they are bound, and they have the right, to embrace and keep it.*

No 748 (2): *Let us start from the very beginning with our Abraham our Father in Faith to trace the start of our Catholic faith.*

We read in the first book of the Bible (*Genesis 12:1-2*)

> *Leave your country, your kindred and*
> *your father's house for a country which*
> *I shall show you;*
> *and I shall make you a great nation.*

> *I shall bless you*
> *and make your name famous;*
> *you are to be blessed!*

A spiritual classic, *The Way of a Pilgrim*, speaks to the hearts of contemporary searchers. It is by an anonymous author, who lived in 19th-century Russia and who tells of his lifelong pilgrimage, a search for a way to get closer to God through prayer. The book begins humbly:

> *By the grace of God I am a Christian,*
> *by my deeds a great sinner,*
> *and by my calling a homeless wanderer of humblest origin,*
> *roaming from place to place.*
> *My possessions consist of a knapsack with dry crusts of bread on my back*
> *and, in my bosom the Holy Bible.*
> *This is all!*

In his book Michael Pinnock writes:

The Russian author reminds all seekers of God that we are pilgrims in a foreign land.

Someday we will have to leave the world forsaking our possessions. For the anonymous pilgrim, a knapsack and dried bread were sufficient for his physical needs; the Bible provides nourishment for his spiritual needs. By travelling simply he uncluttered his life for the journey.

In our more complex and sophisticated world, we could hardly get by with the simple supplies of a 19th-century wanderer. Nonetheless, we are 'strangers in a strange land' who are on a lifelong journey, the ultimate destination of which is in union with God who made and sustains us.

The Christian life is a journey which requires insight, determination and support to keep going. There is always a danger that we will get so distracted by the sights along the way that we forget about our final destination.

Thus the Christian pilgrimage requires clear vision to correctly discern the direction indicators along the way. The Bible provides a vision for the Russian pilgrim; it is still a major source of insight for the Christian journey.

We are given sound advice by St Paul about why we must perse-vere in our faith (Col 1:23): "You must hold fast to faith, be firmly grounded and steadfast in it, unshaken in the hope promised you by the Gospel you have heard. It is the Gospel which has been an-nounced to every creature under heaven."

The existence of God is explained by St Paul in the following way (1 Cor 13:12): "Now we see only reflections in a mirror, mere riddles, but then we shall be seeing face to face. Now I can know only imperfectly; but then I shall know just as fully as I am myself known."

Every human being must wonder at some stage in their life about the hidden presence of God which we somehow sense. This forces us to ask questions about the meaning of life……and death.

Why am I here? Why is there suffering? Why do my loved ones and I have to die? What is the meaning of love?

Questions like this force us to face the issue of God's existence. Most people conclude that God exists. Some, however, maintain that the existence for God cannot be proven, therefore for them, there is no God. The atheists also reject the notion of God because they find suffering and evil in the world incompatible with the ex-istence of a supreme and loving Being.

Between the believers and atheists are the agnostics who claim that we cannot know if there is a God or not. The question of the existence of God makes very little impact on their lives.

Atheists and agnostics -and also self-named believers who are in fact indifferent to spiritual realities- challenge believers to re-consider their belief.

Today's Christian pilgrims also need support. No one can sur-vive without other people. The 19th-century wanderer begged food from others and received spiritual encouragement from many holy people. Today's spiritual pilgrims also need others to sup-port and nourish them on their life's journey. The good news of the Christian life is that those who follow the way of Jesus become members of his body. United to the Lord they derive strength and power from him and their fellow travellers. The inspiration of his life and sacrifice on the cross, his ongoing friendship, his presence to us through other people, all of these, make the journey bearable and even adventurous.

The goal of understanding the Catholic faith should be above all else the love and appreciation for the Lord who lives and guides the faith community.

Protestantism

On 31st October 1517, Martin Luther posted his famous *Ninety-Five Theses or Disputation on the Power of Indulgences* with a letter to the Archbishop of Mainz and he also posted them on the door of All Saint's Church in Wittenburg in accordance with university custom.

This act, meant to promote a disputation on the sale of indulgences, is commonly viewed to be the catalyst for the Protestant Reformation.

He did the Catholic Church and Christianity as a whole an inestimable service. Not only did the repercussions of his actions immediately force the Catholic Church into taking a long, hard look at itself, and so introduce some much-needed reforms at the 1545 Council of Trent, but by 1534 he had already translated the Old and New Testament into German. His value for all future Christians thus lay in his desire to make Christ's teachings and Church doctrine more understandable to the common man. To this end he worked tirelessly in drawing up a catechism (a practice later adopted by the Catholic Church), propagating the idea of lay involvement in education and the use of the vernacular in Church Worship.

Nearly 500 years since Luther first horrified Rome with his pronouncements, Vatican Council ll saw a new stress placed on the importance of the laity in the Church's structural organisation, an insistence on the Bible as a focal point in Catholic worship and the replacement of Latin by the local vernacular.

At the time of the Reformation, there were serious disagreements over priestly celibacy, papal authority and the sacrifice of the Mass.

Lutherans have only two sacraments, Baptism and Eucharist, whereas we Catholics celebrate 7 sacraments, namely Baptism, Confirmation, Eucharist, Reconciliation, Anointing of the Sick, Matrimony and Holy Orders.

The Church has traditionally defined a sacrament as an outward sign instituted by Christ to confer inward grace to a person.

The doctrine of *Sola Scriptura* was also one of the reasons which caused the split between Protestants and Catholics and led to the Reformation. The two major tenets on which the Churches disagreed on were, firstly, that we are justified by faith alone, and secondly, the authority for our religion is scripture alone.

It is an interesting observation that since the Reformation more than 25 000 different Protestant denominations have come into existence, with five new ones being formed every week. Every single one of them claims to be following the Holy Spirit and the plain meaning of Scripture.

The obvious question to ask is: which Church is more correct in their interpretation of the Bible and its teaching?

This viewpoint, say Scott and Kimberley Hahn in their book *Rome Sweet Home – Our Journey to Catholicism*, also highlights the irreconcilable differences between the beliefs of Catholics and Protestants:

St Paul (whom I had thought of as the first Luther) taught in Romans, Galatians and elsewhere that justification was more than a legal decree; it established us in Christ as God's children by grace alone. In fact, I discovered that nowhere did Saint Paul ever teach that we were justified by faith alone! "Sola Fide" was unscriptural!

Scripture teaches about the Word of God, but nowhere does it reduce the Word of God to Scripture alone. In fact, the Bible tells us in many places that God's authoritative Word is to be found in the Church: her tradition (2 Th 2:15; 3:6) as well as her preaching and teaching (1 Peter 1:25; 2 Peter 1:20-21; Mt 18:17).

That's why I think the Bible supports the Catholic principle of "Sola Verbum Dei" (the Word of God alone) rather the Protestant slogan "Sola Scriptura" (Scripture alone).

What Christ did say to Peter was: "Upon this rock, I will build my Church ....and the gates of Hades will not prevail against it'" So it makes more sense to me that Jesus left us with his Church – made up of a Pope, bishops and councils – all of which are needed to administer and interpret Scripture.

This is undeniable proof that the Catholic Church is the first Church established by Christ himself.

But there are unanswered questions that must linger in our minds which may never be answered:

> *What hope is there for a reconciliation between the major Christian faiths?*
>
> *What is the best approach to foster Christian unity?*
>
> *It can't be my church is better than your church.*
>
> *We cannot accept we all believe in the same God, there's really not much difference.*
>
> *Rather, as Catholics, we need to be the best Catholics we can be.*
>
> *Our Protestant brothers and sisters need to be the best they can be in terms of their faith.*
>
> *We all need to be the best Christians we can be within our own particular traditions and beliefs that means being faithful to Christ first.*

Saint Richard of Chichester, who died in 1253, is best known today for a prayer he composed:

> **O most merciful Redeemer, Friend and Brother,**
>
> **May I know Thee more clearly, love Thee more dearly and follow Thee more nearly, day by day.**

That means knowing Him, loving Him, following Him, not wondering or worrying if others are knowing, loving or following Him in exactly the same way as us.

As most Christian families today have family members practicing different faiths it is important for harmony and peace to reign in the home that each person respect and understand the main differences between Catholicism and Protestantism and other religions.

It is important to state that all Christians worship the same God, but the principles of their faith are different.

Five hundred years after the Reformation, there are still painful divisions between Protestants and Catholics. This division had deepened over the centuries through religious conflicts and wars. Today, through 'Reconciled diversity' there is an attempt to reach a better understanding and find common ground between the churches. It is doubtful however whether a new united church will ever be realised and many of the aspects that were reformed by Martin Luther at the time of the Reformation still divide both groups to this day.

The Main Differences Between Catholicism and Protestantism

According to a recent US Religious Landscape Survey conducted by the Pew Forum on Religion & Public Life, there are about half as many Catholics as Protestants in America today. But why do so many make this distinction? Don't both groups hold to essentials of Christian faith, like the deity, death, and the resurrection of Jesus? What is the difference in what Protestants believe and what Catholics believe?

For ordinary folk like you and me, Mikel Del Rosario, a doctoral student in New Testament Studies at Dallas Seminary and adjunct Professor of Apologetics and World Religion at William Jessup University, has listed seven key issues, from the *Table Podcast* series by Dr Darrell Bock, Dr Scott Horrell and Dr Michael Svigel, which continue to distinguish the beliefs and practices between what Protestants believe and what Catholics believe:

1. The Magisterium

The term Magisterium refers to the official teaching body of the Roman Catholic Church.

Dr Horrell explains, *"Usually it's related to ......the large house of cardinals and the leading theologians in the movement; but finally, that all comes under, of course, the Pope himself."*

Besides providing a trusted, unified voice to guide Catholics, this body also allows the church to make official pronouncements on contemporary issues which Scripture might not directly address.

Although there is no equivalent to the Magisterium for Protestants, it's possible to compare Catholic and Protestant views of the role of tradition.

2. Tradition

While Protestants don't view tradition as equal in authority with the Scriptures, the Roman Catholic Church has a different perspective - one which clearly distinguishes itself from Protestant Churches.

As Dr Horrell notes: *"The issue of Sola Scriptura ....versus Scripture plus Tradition is perhaps the fundamental difference between Roman Catholicism and Protestantism... What you're talking about, it's a hermeneutic, a way of doing theology."*

While Protestants view the Scriptures as authoritative only, the Catholic Catechism clearly states that Church: *"...does not derive her certainty about all revealed truths from Holy Scripture alone. Both Scripture and Tradition must be accepted and honoured with equal sentiments of devotion and reverence".*

3. Salvation and Grace

Protestants often express the idea that salvation is by faith alone, through grace alone, in Christ alone. This assertion views justification as a specific point upon which God declares that you are righteous – a point where you enter into the Christian life.

In contrast, the Roman Catholic Church views justification as a process, dependent on the grace you receive by participating in the Church – which is seen as a repository of saving grace.

Dr Svigel explains the Catholic perspective: *'Grace is treated almost as if it's a substance, something that can be dispensed through various avenues of change and means....... You're saved by grace, but how you receive that grace and what that grace does and whether it's a one-time entrance into the Christian life or if it's a constant movement toward salvation – that's really the big difference between Protestantism and the Roman Catholic Church.'*

4. The Eucharist

When it comes to the Eucharist, which most Protestants call *The Lord's Supper* or *Communion*, the Roman Catholic Christian holds to the doctrine of *transubstantiation* - the idea that the edible ritual elements used during the Mass literally become the body and blood of Christ.

Dr Svigel explains: *"At the moment the priest says, 'This is my body' the invisible, unperceivable essence that ......you couldn't see (with) an electron microscope, (is) there is a miracle, it contains, the body, blood, soul and divinity of Christ. And that becomes the spiritual and physical nourishment. As you partake of it, it becomes part of you, transforms you, and makes you more and more righteous."*

In contrast, some Protestants, like Lutherans, hold to a perspective called *consubstantiation* where Jesus' body and blood are seen as coexisting with the bread and the wine. Martin Luther likened this idea to a red-hot iron in a fire united, but not changed.

Dr Bock says: *"I like to call it 'the over, under, around and through' view. Jesus Christ surrounds the elements. He's spiritually present, but he's not in the elements themselves; the elements don't become the body and blood of Christ."*

Still, other Protestants hold to the memorial view – the idea that you're commemorating Jesus' death. In this understanding, the elements are symbols which remain ontologically unaffected by the ritual. (Ontology, introduced in 1606, is the philosophical study of being, becoming, existence or reality).

As previously discussed, Protestants view justification as the moment God declares that a guilty person is righteous because of what Christ has done. Sanctification is the process of being made more righteous throughout your life.

However, Dr Horrell notes that Catholics view justification as both a point and a process:

'What Roman Catholics reject is that there is an imputed righteousness of Christ to us at the moment of salvation, that we are counted as fully righteous in the sight of God'.

6. The Priesthood of All Believers

Rather than a vertical structure, Protestants see the church as having a horizontal structure.

Dr Svigel contrasts the role of the Catholic priest with the Protestant idea of the priesthood of all believers: *'That which is reserved just for the Magisterium, the ability to bind and loose, to forgive and withhold forgiveness through the sacraments and through penance and such, that was just the role of the priest. From Luther on, we have the ability to confess our sins to one another, pronounce forgiveness as the scripture says.'*

7. Veneration of the Saints and the Virgin Mary

Roman Catholics see veneration, not as praying to the Saints and the Virgin Mary, but as praying through them. This is seen as similar to asking a brother or sister in Christ to pray for you.

Dr Svigel adds that the departed saints are also '*able to spill over their over-abundance of grace to us*'.

Furthermore, Dr Horrell notes that the Virgin Mary is seen as '*the Mother of our Lord, and therefore she is Mother of His body, and His body is the Church, so she is the Mother of the Church. He is the creator of all things. So she is the Mother of angels. She is the Mother of humanity, as is sometimes said*'.

Moreover, the Catholic Church has also called her the Queen of Heaven. Historically, Mary was given a less prominent position in Protestantism as a reaction to this emphasis in the Catholic Church. There is no equivalent to this kind of veneration in Protestantism, as Protestants emphasise direct access to God.

Conclusion

While both Protestants and Catholics agree on many essentials of the historic Christian faith, there are key issues which continue to distinguish their beliefs and practices.

Spiritual Reading

According to Archbishop Thomas Menamparamphil SDB in *The Transformative Power of Books*, reading seems to be a lost art in this age of smartphones, social media, video games, Facebook, WhatsApp, Instagram and Skype. It is not his intention to underestimate the wide range of possibilities that these means of communication can offer you. All he wants to insist on is that reading still holds something valuable out to you.

Life appears worthwhile to human beings only as long they are able to give a meaning to their life and assign a purpose to their activities. Reading helps them to do precisely this: to widen their horizon, deepen their reflection, to make intelligent choices, and arrive at purposeful conclusions.

The information that reading provides enlightens your mind, and the motivation it generates not only keeps you hale and hearty but also supplies you with energies you require to strive after goals that you set before yourself.

According to Francis Bacon, philosopher, statesman, scientist, jurist *(1561-1626):*

Reading maketh a full man, a ready man and writing an exact man. Knowledge is power. In order for light to shine so brightly, the darkness must be present.

Spiritual reading in the busyness of our daily activities – work, meetings, household chores, shopping, socialising, medical checkups, reading, watching TV and whatever keeps you busy - is as important that you as part of your many daily routines in the morning – showering, shaving, exercise, applying makeup, having breakfast and checking messages. Set a little time aside for prayer and inspirational readings to put you in touch with God for the day ahead.

It should become a life-long habit, as it is very easy to fall by the wayside in your faith. We are all creatures of habit so you soon find that by persevering, you increase your faith and acceptance of your reliance on God and not your own efforts.

Here is an example taken from *mediations@mysoulprovider. org* (but there many other daily readings which you may find you like on the internet and in publications) how such a daily reading can inspire you and direct your thoughts for the day ahead in the right way with relatively no real effort on your side – except the commitment, desire and realisation that, after all, this is why we are put on earth!

Never the Twain Shall Meet

It is sad to witness a person who has had faith lose it. It happens. Usually, it is a slow process, just a little laziness here and there, the quiet indulgence in secret of substances that are best left alone. Always there is self-justification and excuses that seem to make it alright. And always the promise that 'One day I'll sort it out'. The Galatians had lost their faith and were cutting themselves off from Christ in the process.

Salvation by grace and salvation by works (or the Law) don't go together. They focus on two mutually exclusive attitudes. People who go the way of salvation by works focus on themselves, what they are doing, and how much good they are doing to other people. Their lives are a matter of ticking a scorecard. But it all focuses on their achievements.

Because the focus is on themselves they are sure to come a crop-

per one day. And deep down inside they develop a sense of guilt because they know they haven't achieved perfection.

Salvation by grace, by contrast, is all about what God has done. People who are saved by grace think and talk about Christ and what He has done. Their thinking centres, not on the effort they are making to do well, but on gratitude to God in Christ for what Christ has done and what He is doing now. They do very little spiritual 'navel-gazing' because Jesus is their all-in-all.

Don't rely on your 'scorecard'. It doesn't mean a thing. Only your own relationship with Jesus counts – but His grace can't be counted.

Those of you who try to be put right with God by obeying the Law have cut yourselves from Christ. (Galatians 5:4).

Soul Search:

When you can do the common things of life in an uncommon way, you will command the attention of the world. (George Washington).

Life Tips:

The key to quality in life is in the choices we make every day.

Prayer Thought:

Lord, help me to forget my scorecard and focus on Christ alone.

Now that didn't take you too long to read, be honest with yourself, no more than a minute or two. Ideally, you should read it slowly again and see how this affects the way you live your life.

The real benefit is that the reading is embedded in your subconscious mind and there is an awareness and interest to think about other important issues. During the day ahead you will contemplate how some of this impacts on your life. You can't but be a better person as you will be guided how to live a more meaningful life in the busyness of daily living.

Try it! You will never regret it.

The Ups and Downs of Faith

You have managed to read this far so you are no doubt serious about your faith or intrigued to know more about the ins and outs of faith, which for all of us is an integral part of our life on earth.

This is what Fr Ron Rolheiser OMI had to say in a recent article in his column *Final Reflections*:

*I give you this wonderful practical explanation of what to ex-
pect in your journey of faith.*

*The poet Rumi suggests that we live with a deep secret that
sometimes we know, then not, and then know again.*

*That's a good description of faith. Faith isn't something you nail
down or possess once and for all. It goes this way: Sometimes you
walk on water and sometimes you sink like a stone.*

*The Gospels testify to this, most graphically, in the story of Peter
walking on the water. Jesus asks Peter to step out of the boat and
walk across the water to him. At first, it works, and Peter, unthink-
ing, walks on the water- then, becoming more conscious of what
he is doing, he sinks like a stone.*

*We see this too in the massive fluctuations in belief that Jesus'
disciples experience during the 40 days after the Resurrection.
Jesus would appear to them, they would trust he was alive, then
he would disappear again, and they would lose their trust and go
back to the lives they'd led before they had met him, fishing and
the sea.*

*The post-Resurrection narratives illustrate the dynamics of
faith pretty clearly: You believe it. Then you distrust. Then you believe it again. At least, so it seems on the surface. We see another
example of this in the story of Peter betraying Jesus.*

*In Mark's Gospel, Jesus tells us that there is a secret which sep-
arates those have faith from those who don't: 'To you is given the
secret of the kingdom, but to those outside everything exists in
parables.'*

*That sounds like Gnosticism, that is, the idea that there's a se-
cret code somewhere (for example, the book and film* The Da Vinci
Code*) that some know and some don't, and you are in or out depending on whether you know it or not.*

*But that's not what Jesus is saying here. His secret is an open
one, accessible to all: the meaning of the cross. Anyone who understands this will understand the rest of what Jesus means, and vice
versa. We are in or out, depending upon whether or not we can
grasp and accept the meaning of Jesus' death.*

But, being in or out isn't once and for all things. Rather, we move in and out! After Peter denied Jesus, we're told: he went outside. This is intended both literally and metaphorically. After his denial, Peter stepped outside a gate into the night to be away from the crowd, but he also stepped outside the meaning of his faith.

Our faith also bounces up and down for another reason- we misunderstand how it works. Take, for example, the rich young man who approaches Jesus with this question: "Good Master, what must I do to possess eternal life?" That's an interesting choice of a verb: to "possess". Eternal life as a possession?

Jesus' gentle correction of the young man's verb teaches us something vital about faith.

Jesus says to him: "Now if you wish to receive eternal life", meaning that faith and eternal life are not something you possess so that they can be stored and guarded like grain in a silo, money in a bank, or jewellery in a box. They can only be received, like the air we breathe.

Air is free, is everywhere, and our health doesn't depend on its presence, for it's always there, but rather on the state of our lungs (and mood) at any given moment. Sometimes we breathe deeply and appreciatively; but sometimes, for various reasons, we breathe badly, gasp for breath, are out of breath or are choking for air. Like breathing, faith too has its modalities.

And so we need to understand our faith, not as a possession or as something we achieve once and for all, which can be lost only by some huge, dramatic, life-changing shift inside of us, where we move from belief to atheism.

The 20ᵗʰ-century Rabbi Abraham Herschel suggests: "Faith isn't some constant state of belief, but rather a sort of faithfulness, a loyalty to the moments when we've had faith".

And that teases out something else: To be real, faith need not be explicitly religious, but can also express itself simply in faithfulness, loyalty, and trust.

For example, in a powerful memoir written when she was dying of cancer, *The Bright Hour*, Nina Riggs shares her strong but implicit faith as she bravely faces her death.

Not given to explicit religious faith, she is challenged at one point by a nurse who says to her: *'Faith, you gotta have it, and you're gonna need it!'*

The comment triggers a reflection on Riggs's part about what she does or doesn't believe in. She comes to peace with the question and for her own stake in it with these words:

For me faith involves staring into the abyss, seeing that it is dark and full of the unknown – and being okay with that.

Faith is deeper than our feelings.

We need to trust the unknown, knowing that we will be okay, no matter that on a given day we might feel like we are walking on water or sinking like a stone. *Faith is deeper than our feelings.*

You'll Never Walk Alone

This famous song, which was the show tune from the 1945 Rogers and Hammerstein musical *Carousel*, is sung at football matches around the world. The tradition began after the chart success of the 1963 single of the song by the local Liverpool group *Gerry and the Pacemakers*. Fans get very emotional every time at the mass rendition of Liverpool F C's signature tune by supporters.

The background of the song is very moving. In the second act of the musical, Nettie Fowler, the cousin of the protagonist Julie Jordan, sings "*You'll Never Walk Alone*" to comfort Julie when her husband, Billy Bigelow, the male lead, falls on his knife and dies after a failed robbery attempt. It is reprised in the final scene to encourage a graduation class of which their daughter Louise is a member. The now invisible Billy, who was granted the chance to return to Earth for one day to redeem himself, watches the ceremony and is able to silently motivate the unhappy Louise to join in the song.

Here are the words of this inspirational song so that you can join in the singing instead of just humming when you hear this classic football anthem sung by the fans at the top of the lungs:

When you walk through a storm
Hold your head up high
And don't be afraid of the dark.
At the end of the storm
Is a golden sky
And the sweet silver song of a lark
Walk on through the wind

Walk on through the rain
Though your dreams be tossed and blown.
Walk on walk on with hope in your heart
And you'll never walk alone.
You'll never walk alone.
Walk on walk on with hope in your heart
And you'll never walk alone.

In a way, these words express our faith in living out our daily lives. That's most probably why so many ordinary people the world over, who readily profess not to be very religious, can find meaning in these words.

Footprints in the Sand

In much the same way the words of an equally famous poem, written by Mary Stevenson in 1936, help us in our journey of faith especially when we feel all alone, frightened and abandoned in our quiet moments. A person cannot but be inspired and encouraged to carry on knowing that we never need to be alone.

One night I dreamed a dream.
As I was walking along the beach with my Lord,
across the dark sky flashed scenes from my life.
For each scene, I noticed two sets of footprints in the sand.
One belonging to me and one to my Lord.
After the last scene of my life flashed before me,
I looked back at the footprints in the sand.
I noticed that many times along the path of my life,
especially at the very lowest and saddest times,
there was only one set of footprints.
This really troubled me, so I asked the Lord about it.
'Lord, you said once I decided to follow You,
You'll walk with me all the way.
But I noticed that during the saddest and most troublesome
times of my life,
there was only one set of footprints.
I don't understand why, when I needed You the most,
You would leave me'.
He whispered, 'My precious child, I love you

and will never leave you,
never, ever, during your trials and testings.
When you saw only one set of footprints,
it was then that I carried you.'

The Imitation of Christ

Next to the Bible, *De Imitiatione Christi* by Thomas a Kempis (1340 – 1471) is among the most famous religious works of the Christian world, translated into more than fifty languages and printed in more 6 000 editions. Published in about 1420, the first English translation appeared in 1696.

Did you know that a well-known saying *"Man proposes, God disposes"* is a quote from *The Imitation of Christ*?

The basic message of *The Imitation of Christ* is that God is everything and humanity is nothing without God.

Therefore, humanity must strive for the eternal truth of God by imitating the spirit and actions of Jesus Christ who is the full revelation of God because he is God's son. There's nothing new in this, of course. We know it from the Bible and Church teaching.

The greatness of Thomas a Kempis' book is its literary genius, that is, the way it brings together many strands of Christian literature in a simple and practical way. It has sometimes been described as a "mosaic" of ideas taken from the Bible, from the writings of the Church fathers, and from the early and medieval Christian mystics such as Saints Bernard, Gregory, Ambrose, and Thomas Aquinas. Even the philosophers like Plato, Aristotle and Seneca can be found within its pages. Yet despite the external sources that he draws on, the wisdom and personal sincerity of Thomas a Kempis himself shines through, drawing the reader into his own obvious devotion of Christ.

Thomas a Kempis is quite practical in his insights into human beings, in other words, what makes us "tick", our complexities and mixed motives. He shows that virtue can only be claimed by those who know about struggle and temptation and have proved themselves equal to the challenge. One must have experienced temptation in order to remain a follower of Christ's doctrines and example.

Here are some thoughts of his to ponder on:

> *Be not angry that you cannot make others as you wish them to be, since you cannot make yourself as you wish to be.*
>
> *First keep peace within yourself, then you can also bring peace to others.*
>
> *If God were your only desire, you would not be so upset when your opinions aren't accepted.*
>
> *As long as you live you will be subject to change, whether you like it or not.*
>
> *God wills that we learn to bear one another's burdens; for no-one is without fault. No-one is sufficient unto him/herself, wise enough of him/herself. So we ought to bear with one another, comfort one another, help and instruct one another.*

Thomas a Kempis encourages the practice of setting aside time in silence for prayer and deep personal reflection. *Ja well no fine*, we might say, in the face of the busy lives we have, getting children ready for school, getting through heavy traffic to work, taking public transport, and everything in between. Then too there are the invasive distractions of television, the internet and social media.

The wisdom of Thomas a Kempis is that he helps us to distinguish between saying prayers and praying. Prayer is simply the ability to stop and take a deep breathe, to turn inwards, no matter how briefly and be aware of God, more with an attitude of listening than of doing all the talking.

Here's what Thomas a Kempis says:

I will hear what the Lord God will speak in me. Blessed is the one who hears the Lord speaking within, who receives word of consolation from God's lips. Blessed are the ears that catch the accents of divine whispering and pay no heed to the murmurings of this world. Blessed indeed are the ears that listen, not to the voice which sounds without, but to the truth which teaches within. Blessed are the eyes which are closed to exterior things and are fixed upon those which are interior.

So prayer is going within, in silence, there to encounter God. Some readers of the publication *The Link* have met or know about the South African Redemptorist, Father Cyril Axelrod, who was born and raised Jewish and is both deaf and blind. Each of those faculties functioned when he went to a synagogue to pray for a Jewish friend, chanting the Jewish *Shema* –

> *Hear/listen Israel,*
> *The Lord your God is one ...*

After Cyril had prayed, the rabbi commented: *"When we Jews chant the Shema, we have to close our eyes and go within. This man is blessed. He is in a permanent state of Shema."*

Close the door of your senses, so that you can hear what the Lord your God speaks within you. We are invited to seek our 'still centre', not to find inner peace for its own sake, but to find God. This requires letting go of ideas about what we are supposed to achieve and instead listen to the words: *"Be still and know I am your God."*

Prayer means to let go (especially our never-ending requests) and simply allow God to carry us. God already knows our needs

This prayer by Thomas a Kempis might help you to pray:

> *Grant us O Lord, to know what I ought to know,*
> *to love what I ought to love*
> *to praise what delights You most,*
> *to value what is precious in Your sight,*
> *to hate what grieves You.*
> *Do not allow me to judge according to the sight of my eyes,*
> *but to discern with true judgment between things*
> *visible and spiritual*
> *and above all,*
> *always to inquire Your Holy will.*

Rejoice and Be Glad

In Pope Francis' new Apostolic Exhortation *Rejoice And Be Glad (Gaudete et Exsultate)* it clear that Christians cannot strive for holiness with prayer alone, but must aim at serving those most in need, particularly those who risk their lives for the future of their children.

In this 98-page document, the Pope focuses on how Christians could be holy in today's world emphasising that the most basic teaching handed on by Jesus was to help others *without any ifs or buts.*

The Exhortation, released on 9th April 2018, is a reflection of the great criteria Jesus said would be used at the final judgement: *"I was hungry and you gave me no food, I was thirsty and you gave me no drink, I was a stranger and you did not welcome me."*

The Pope repeatedly stresses the need for Christians to both pray and serve others. He cites the question St Thomas asked in his *Summa Theologie* after reflecting deeply on the meaning of the great criteria: *"What actions by man best showed God's love?"* He again quotes from St Thomas: *"We worship God by outward sacrifices and gifts, not for His own benefit, but for that of ourselves and our neighbour. "*

The pontiff criticises Christians who focus on one ethical issue, such as abortion, over and above all others, calling that a *'harmful ideological error'*. He reaffirms Catholic opposition to abortion saying: *"It needs to be clear, firm and passionate, for at stake is the dignity of human life, which is always sacred. Equally sacred, however, are the lives of the poor, those already born, the destitute, the abandoned and the underprivileged.*

"We cannot uphold an ideal of holiness that would ignore injustice in a world where some revel, spend with abandon and live only for the latest consumer goods, even as others look on from afar, living their entire lives in abject poverty."

He asks all Christians not to omit, in dialogue with the Lord, a sincere daily examination of conscience. Listening to God in prayer means being open to change, even when changes are surprising or go against the grain. Entailed obedience to the Gospel is the ultimate standard, as also is the Magisterium that guards it.

The pontiff explains how people could grow in holiness, quoting the example of a woman who goes shopping, meets a friend and is tempted to gossip but does not. She then goes home and wants to rest, but her child wants to speak to her. She listens instead of resting.

"This is a step to holiness... one step at a time. You too need to see the entirety of your life as a mission. Try to do so by listening to God in prayer and recognizing the signs he gives you. Always ask the Spirit what Jesus expects from you at every moment of your life and every decision you must make."

He frequently addresses the reader individually throughout the text as "you", and asks direct questions meant to help each person to examine their own quest for holiness.

Here is a lovely summary of key quotes from *Gaudete et Exsultate* which is very helpful in appreciating the very personal concern of the pontiff for each member of his church:

- I *like to contemplate the holiness present in the patience of God's people: In those parents who raise their children with immense love, in those men and women who work hard to support their families, in the sick, in elderly religious who never lose their smile.*
- *Holiness is the most attractive face of the Church.*
- *We are all called to be holy by living our lives with love and by bearing witness in everything we do, wherever we find ourselves.*
- *This holiness to which the Lord calls you will grow through small gestures.*
- *-Do not be afraid of holiness. It will take away none of your energy, vitality or joy.*
- *Giving and forgiving means reproducing in our lives some small measure of God's perfection, which gives and forgives superabundantly.*
- *We need to think of ourselves as an army of the forgiven. All of us have been looked upon with divine compassion.*
- *It is true the primacy belongs to our relationship with God, but we cannot forget that our ultimate criterion on which our lives will be judged is what we have done for others.*

The Three Little Catholics of St Agapantha's

I read this article written by Fr Roger Hickley, Parish priest in Hermanus, which i found the pile of papers in my study some years ago. Behind the amusing, very human story of what you find in every parish all over the world, there is a sombre message for each one of us. The real test of our faith is to see how the nine fruits of the Holy Spirit impact us in our daily lives. After all is said and done, the real challenge facing us is to answer one simple question:

Is His love an important part of your and your family's life?

We humans all fail dismally in this vital area of enjoying and living life to the fullest as God intended. But we simply must keep on trying for it is never too late to love.

Once upon a timeless moment in heaven, the Lord Jesus, having time on His hands and time in His hands, decided it was really high time He had a word with the three little Catholics of St Agapantha's. But before He does so, I want to tell you about them. Their names were: Mrs Church-drilled, Mr Self-skilled and Miss Spirit-filled. This is what they were like.

The first little Catholic, Mrs Church-drilled, never missed going to Mass and the Sacraments. She obeyed the laws of the Church and accepted all its teachings. Her public life revolved around St Agapantha's Parish and her private prayers revolved around the Rosary. She always sat at the very front of the church and she always prayed with her hands carefully clasped together. She had great patience and great self-control.

(Strictly between you and me, she had no time for Mr Self-skilled or for Miss Spirit-filled).

She had noticed that Mr Self-skilled was not as scrupulously regular at attending Mass as herself. He was overheard making critical remarks about the parish and even about her beloved parish priest. Mr Self-skilled never came to Wednesday devotions (needless to say) and on the irregular Sundays that he did attend church, he always sat at the very back praying (was he praying or dozing?) with his arms folded across his chest.

As for Miss Spirit-filled, well, Mrs Church-drilled was even less enthusiastic about her. She claimed to speak in tongues, which Mrs Church-drilled knew perfectly well was a lot of nonsense. She was always going on about her 'prayer group' and about 'sharing charisms' and about 'Renewal'. She seemed to sit in a different place at every Mass and, on a few shocking occasions, Mrs Church had personally witnessed her praying (was she praying or raving?) with her arms above her head!

The second little Catholic, Mr Self-skilled, certainly believed in God and tried to pray. Some of the Church's teaching he liked so he obeyed; but others - especially those about sex - he disliked, so he disobeyed, preferring his own reasoning powers to the Church's authority. What drove him was a great urge to build the Gospel kingdom of justice and peace. Change and social action were what he wanted to see if he and everyone else were to find fulfillment in life: changes in the Church and changes in society. He wanted to help in a practical way and kept saying to himself: 'I must do more for people'. He had great kindness and goodness.

Again (strictly between you and me) he had no time at all for Mrs Church-drilled or for Miss Spirit-filled. The former he found so hopelessly old-fashioned, outdated and pre-Vatican II. With her it was always 'Yes, Father', 'No, Father', 'Just as you say, Father'. As for Miss Spirit-filled, he had rather fancied her once and even asked her out a few times but she had what she called 'the Baptism of the Spirit' and, after that, she kept wanting him to come to prayer meetings, and clap his hands, and say 'Praise the Lord' all over the place.

The third little Catholic, Miss Spirit-filled, had truly been having the most wonderful time since she was prayed over by a charismatic preacher. She told everyone at St Agapantha's how she had now accepted Jesus as her personal Lord and Saviour: how her palms went all hot when she laid hands on people; and how the Spirit really moved at prayer meetings. Mass was, by contrast, so dry and dead, and Father was painfully un-renewed. How thrilled and blessed she felt with all these new charisms. She had great trustfulness and joy.

But (keeping this to yourself of course) she had no time for Mrs Church-drilled or Mr Self-skilled.

"Well, I'm not trying to be unkind, praise the Lord, but sMrs Church-drilled simply hasn't opened herself up to be renewed, so I'm just praying she'll be born again in the Spirit."

Ask her about Mr Shelf-skilled: "You know, I went out with him once but then the Lord spoke to me and told me not to have anything to do with him. The Lord said he's too worldly and that I mustn't even speak to him. Alleluia! Thank you, Jesus!"

So there they were the three little Catholics of St Agapantha's. Now, the day the Lord decided to have a word with them just happened to be St Agapantha's Feast Day, a time of particular solemnity in the parish on earth and a timelessness of particular gaiety in the courts of heaven.

"Happy Feast Day," said the Lord to St Agapantha. *"What shall I say to out three little Catholics down there in your parish? I've decided it's high time I have a word with them."*

"Good Lord!" exclaimed St Agapantha and, putting down her feast-day harp (on eternal loan from St Cecilia), she parted the clouds and carefully examined the pews at Sunday Mass.

Mrs Church-drilled was at the very front. Mr Self-filled was at the back and Miss Spirit-filled was somewhere in the middle. They were listening to the Scripture readings chosen for the day: the First Reading from Galatians about the fruits of the Holy Spirit being Love, Joy, Peace, Patience, Kindness, Goodness, Trustfulness, Gentleness and Self-control: and then the Gospel, about our Lord washing the disciples' feet.

When they all sat down after the Gospel St Agapantha had a sudden inspiration. She turned to the Lord and said: "Mrs Church-drilled has such loyalty and obedience to your Holy Church, and she is so persevering in her faith. She has the fruits of the Spirit named Patience and Self-control and with these, she has so much to offer Mr Self-skilled and Miss Spirit-filled. Mr Self-skilled, on the other hand, has such eagerness and practical concern to make your kingdom come to everyone, and he does much good. He has the fruits of the Spirit called Kindness and Goodness, and with these, he has so much to offer Mrs Church-drilled and Miss Spirit-filled. And Lord, Miss Spirit-filled burns with such a Pentecostal fire to share with others her personal experience of being loved and forgiven and saved by You. She has the fruits of the Spirit called Trustfulness and Joy, and with these, she has so much to offer Mrs Church-drilled and Mr Self-skilled. But..." St Agapantha *stopped and then added, with a heavenly frown, "Lord there are three other fruits of the Spirit in Galatians."*

"I know," said the Lord very quietly. *"And what about the washing of the feet?"*

"It's really high time you had a word with them," replied St Agapantha.

And so the Lord Jesus walked up the aisle of St Agapantha's Church during Sunday Mass. He gently unclasped the hands of Mrs Church-drilled and He gently unfolded the arms of Mr Self-skilled and He gently lowered the raised arms of Miss Spirit-filled.

Then He joined their hands together, covering them with His own wounded hands, saying with an infinite tenderness: "I love each one of you and, if you love Me, you will forgive and accept one another, and wash one another's feet. And then, the Holy Spirit will give to each one of you, the three remaining fruits: Gentleness, Peace and the best of all, Love."

Suddenly in heaven, St Agapantha found the lost chord on her harp! And she laughed musically as she prayed for the three little Catholics who, once upon a time, tried to live happily ever after.

Noontime for the Church

Looking ahead amid the uncertainties in the world today and my own serious questioning about how faith will be practiced by the generations to come, I found this thought-provoking article by Fr Ron Rolheiser OMI which I have reproduced verbatim as it helped me to a better understanding and assisted in allaying my fears on the challenges that lie ahead for the Catholic Church, in fact for the whole of Christianity.

There is a popular notion which suggests that it can be helpful to compare every century of Christianity's existence to one year of life. That would make Christianity 21 years old - a young 21, grown-up, enough to exhibit a basic maturity but still far from a finished product.

How insightful is this notion? That's a complex question because Christianity expresses itself in communities of worship and in spiritualities that vary greatly across the world.

For instance, just to speak of Church, it is difficult to speak of the Christian Church in any global way: In Africa, for the most part, the churches are young, full of young life, and exploding with growth, with all the strengths and problems that come with that.

In Eastern Europe, the churches are still emerging from the long years of oppression under Communism, and are struggling now to find a new balance and new energy within an ever-intensifying secularity.

Latin American churches have given us liberation theology for a reason. There the issues of social injustice and those advocating for it in Jesus' name and those reacting against them have deeply coloured how Church and spirituality are lived and understood.

In Asia, the situation is even more complex. One might talk of four separate ecclesial expressions and corresponding spiritualities in Asia: There is Buddhist Asia, Hindu Asia, Muslim Asia, and a seeming post-Christian Asia. Churches and spiritualities express themselves quite differently in these parts of Asia.

Finally, there is still Western Europe and North America, the so-called "West", but which appears from the most outward appearances to be aged, grey-haired, and tired - an exhausted project.

How accurate is this picture of Christianity in the Western World, North America and other highly secularist parts of the world? Are we, as churches, old, tired, grey-headed, and exhausted?

That's one view, but the picture admits of other interpretations.

Sigmund Freud and Karl Marx, along with many Enlightenment figures, saw Christianity as a spent project, as a dying reality, its demise the inevitable death of childhood naïveté.

But the Jesuit Pierre Teilhard de Chardin, looking at the same evidence, saw things in exactly the opposite way. For him, Christianity was still in nappies, struggling still to grow to maturity, a child still learning to walk; hence its occasional stumbles.

Contemporary spiritual writer Tomas Halik, the recent winner of the prestigious Templeton Award, suggests still another picture. For Halik, Christianity in the West is undergoing a noon-day fatigue, a writer's block, a crisis of imagination.

Twelve years after his conversion, St Augustine sat down to write about his life in his *Confessions of St Augustine*.

His genius was to open his heart in a way that millions of people have been able to identify with both in terms of wellness and of the gift of mercy and reconciliation. Who cannot identify with his heartfelt cry: *"Late I have loved Thee, O Beauty, so ancient and so new; late have I loved Thee."*

However, faith must not be an add-on to our daily lives but an integral part of living our lives to the fullest. In fact, recent medical scientific studies show that faith, liturgy, and prayer increases healing. God reveals Himself not just through scripture and tradition but also through nature.

At Lourdes, the sacred place of healing, we are challenged by St Augustine's words: *"Miracles are not contrary to nature, but only contrary to what we know about nature."*

All this deep theology is challenging and, it must be freely acknowledged, beyond the thinking of the average Catholic whose faith is largely evidenced by dutifully attending Mass on Sunday. But this critical analysis of the state of our faith is necessary to see the new role of the Church in the modern world in order to bring Christ back into our daily lives, rather continuing the trend of moving further away, which does not bode well for even for our secular world.

The Diaconate

It was for this reason that Lynne and I become acutely aware that our parish of St Joseph's needed the greater involvement of the laity. We responded to a request by Fr Tony Kelly, our parish priest at the time, to assist him at Mass by becoming Extraordinary Ministers of the Eucharist.

Later we decided to attend a three-year part-time Theology course run by a Jesuit priest, Fr Michael Austin, at St David's College in Sandton. This was followed by a year's specialised course in Homiletics and later Pastoral Counselling training sessions at Holy Trinity Church in Braamfontein ,run by the Jesuits. Our class practiced delivering homilies from the pulpit under the expert guidance of Fr Emil Blaser OP, who founded Radio Veritas in Edenvale, the only Catholic Radio station in Southern Africa. This was followed by the Acolyte, Lectorlyte and finally ordination as a Permanent Deacon by Archbishop Buti Thlagale at Christ the King Cathedral in Johannesburg on 30th April 2011.

To be perfectly honest it was never my intention to become a deacon, but looking back. I realise that God works in mysterious ways. He turns a simple seed into a mighty tree and a lowly caterpillar into a beautiful butterfly! Who knows what wonders He is accomplishing right now beyond our notice? In times when we think He is doing nothing, He is already accomplishing something beautiful and great! Quietly, He does His work, closing doors that would harm us, paving a way even through the desert to make a way for us, protecting us beyond our knowledge.

I found this very old lovely poem which I read in a reflective mood and it made me realise that the answer to the purpose of your life is coming. It may not arrive at the time or way you want, but if you keep your faith, it will definitely come at the perfect moment. It will not only satisfy you, but it will also astound you!

God Moves in a Mysterious Way was written by William Cowper in 1774.

> *God moves in a mysterious way*
> *His wonders to perform*
> *He plants His footsteps in the sea*
> *and rides upon the storm.*
> *Deep in unfathomable mines*
> *of never-failing skill*
> *He treasures up His bright designs*
> *and works His sov'reign will.*
> *Ye fearful saints fresh courage take;*
> *The clouds ye so much dread*
> *are big with mercy and shall break*
> *in blessings on your head.*
> *Judge not the Lord by feeble sense;*
> *But trust Him for His grace;*
> *Behind a frowning providence*
> *He hides a smiling face.*
> *His purposes will ripen fast,*
> *upholding every hour:*
> *The bud may have a bitter feast,*
> *But sweet will be the flow'r.*
> *Blind unbelief is sure to err*
> *and scan His work in vain;*
> *God is His own interpreter,*
> *and He will make it plain.*

So this the story of how I become to be ordained a deacon in the Catholic Church.

In the third year of our Theology course, round about the middle of the year, I approached Fr Michael Austin, the presenter of the course, at the end of a class to request that, as Lynne and I were going to visit our family in New Jersey for four weeks, could he give me an outline of the lectures we would miss and any notes he had prepared. This would be much appreciated so that on our return we could resume classes.

His response was that this was not to his liking and he suggested that we could attend classes in two years' time when this particular subject was again being covered. I was a little taken aback but accepted the situation, as the thought had never entered my mind to go further in my studies to become a deacon. It was then, and will always be, my view that family comes first and then the Church.

To my utter amazement, at the end of that year, Fr Austin read out the candidates he considered suitable to continue their studies towards the diaconate. Lo and behold, my name was read out first. Either he had had a change of heart or had completely forgotten about his earlier decision that I must come back in two years' time!

But there were more obstacles to overcome in the years ahead. I attended the compulsory classes for the next two years on the practical side of involvement in parish life - how to conduct a baptism, a marriage ceremony and a funeral service, how to prepare homilies, how to counsel in various situations and generally how to run a parish, assisting the priest in charge. Archbishop Buti Thlagale agreed on the date of our ordination at the end of 2009. We attended two ceremonies with the bishop to receive our commissioning as Acolytes (to assist the priest at Mass) and Lectorlytes (to read the Gospel and give homilies at Mass, only when asked by the priest).

I tasked Lynne to source the liturgical vestments to be worn at Mass as a deacon. The wearing of vestments used at Mass have a two-fold purpose, according to the General Instruction on the Roman Missal # 335: *These should, therefore, symbolise the function of each ministry. But at the same time the vestments should also contribute to the beauty of the rite.*

The liturgical vestments worn at Mass have evolved over time. Nevertheless, since the earliest days of the Church, liturgical vestments have been worn by priests (and deacons) for the celebration of the Mass. After the legalisation of Christianity in A.D. 313, the Church continued to refine who wore what, when and how until about the year 800 when liturgical norms for vesting were basically standardised and would remain so until the renewal following the Second Vatican Council in 1964.

As many Catholics, and even more so other people, know very little about the different vestments worn, their practical purpose and spiritual significance, here is a brief explanation of the investments worn at Mass:

- The amice is a piece of white linen, rectangle in shape, with two long cloth ribbons. It is placed around the neck, covering the clerical collar, and then tied by crisscrossing the ribbons in the front (to form a St Andrew's cross), bringing them around the back, around the waist and tied in a bow. The practical purpose of the amice is to conceal the normal clerical clothing of the wearer and to absorb any perspiration from the head and neck. The spiritual purpose is to remind the priest of St Paul's admonition: *Take the helmet of salvation and the sword of the spirit, the Word (Ephesians 6:17).*

- The alb is a long white garment, which flows from the shoulders to ankles, and has long sleeves extending to the wrist, similar to the soutane worn in the Middle East. The spiritual purpose reminds the priest of his baptism, when he was clothed in white to signify his freedom from sin, purity of new life, and Christian dignity. Moreover, the Book of Revelation describes the saints who stand around the altar of the Lamb in Heaven as *these are the ones who have survived the great period of trial; they have washed their robes and washed them white in the blood of the Lamb (Revelation 7:14)*

- The cincture is a long, thick cord with tassels the ends which secures the alb around the waist. It may be white or may be the same liturgical colour as the other vestments. Spiritually, the cincture reminds the priest of the admonition of St Peter: *So gird the loins of your understanding; live soberly; set all your hope on the gift to be conferred on you when Jesus Christ appears. As obedient sons, do not yield to the desires that once shaped you in your ignorance. Rather, become Holy yourselves in every aspect of your conduct, after the likeness of the Holy One who called you (1 Peter: 13-15).*

- The Stole is a long cloth, about four inches wide and the same colour as the chasuble that is worn around the neck like a scarf. The stole too is of ancient origin. Rabbis wore prayer shawls with tassels as a sign of their authority. The crisscrossing of the stole also was symbolic of the crisscrossed belts the Roman soldiers wore: one belt, holding the sword at the waist, and the other belt, holding the pouch with provisions, like food and water. In this sense, the stole reminds the priest not only of his authority and dignity as a priest, but also of his duty to preach the Word of God with courage and conviction: *Indeed, God's Word is living and effective, sharper than any two-edged sword* (*Hebrews 4:12*).

- Finally, the chasuble is the outer garment worn over the alb and stole. It protected the person from inclement weather. Spiritually, the chasuble reminds the priest of the charity of Christ: *Over all these virtues put on love, which binds the rest together and makes them perfect* (*Colossians 3:4*). The colour of the chasuble changes for the different seasons of the church year – green (ordinary time), red (Lord's passion, Palm Sunday, Pentecost, martyrs), white (Christmas, Easter, Feasts of the Lord), violet (advent and funerals), and rose (Gaudete Sunday).

Again there were more hiccups to come in my ordination as a deacon.

Our parish priest, Fr Maurice Kelly, was recalled to Ireland, where his Religious Order had their House, because of ill health. He had spent 40 years in Nigeria as a missionary priest in very remote parts of the country. As he was more than 80 years of age and needed a hip replacement, he was ordered to return to Ireland for an operation, much to his dismay as he loathed the rainy weather back home. Sadly he was never to return to Africa, which he loved because of the sunny skies and its people.

Monsignor John Finlayson was then appointed our parish priest. As he was newly appointed he felt that he needed time to know me better, so he thought that my ordination should be delayed until a later date. I wasn't too unhappy with his decision. In fact, I welcomed it as my son Graeme and I were in the throes of a lengthy criminal and civil case which had dragged on for more than 10 years and was only concluded in our favour in 2013.

My real concern at the time was that that there could be adverse publicity for the Catholic Church if the court decision went against us, even though we were confident that we had not committed any crime in signing audit reports for a client to obtain loan finance. These false accusations and long drawn out legal matters had seriously affected my confidence and were mentally draining.

A new issue arose when our newly appointed director for Deacons, Fr Phillip Miller, discovered that there was a policy decision of the Bishop that a deacon must be ordained by the age of 60. The problem was that I was already 71! When I was informed about this, I shrugged my shoulders and thought this was the final nail in the coffin. I didn't even raise an objection as to why my name had been put forward for the diaconate in the first place. Somehow this oversight was accepted but hopefully, the calling and training of future deacons will be done on a more professional business-like manner in order to attract dedicated laity as future potential leaders in the Church.

Understandably, I began to think that it was not to be that I be ordained a deacon. Maybe God was telling me something. With this doubt in my mind I decided to donate the money saved for the vestments for my ordination to Little Eden, a home for hand-icapped children, that I had been involved with for many years, to purchase some items - spiral candle stands, a monstrance and a thurible and incense boat for their new chapel at Elvia Rota Village.

I attended the my class' Deaconal Ordination Mass at Christ the King Cathedral to celebrate with them and their families and to show support to my classmates with whom I had spent many years in training for the diaconate. As I sat in the pews with the large joyful congregation I was very happy for them but still felt a twinge of regret that I was not there with them.

The next year was largely spent in preparing for our defence in the criminal case and the civil matter. We attended court 42 times from the start to the conclusion of our ordeal. The Scorpions and the Public Prosecutor and the Industrial Development Corporation breached every rule of the South African justice system in order to obtain a conviction against us.

At the end of our lengthy ordeal with the law, I came to two conclusions: Firstly there is something seriously rotten in our beloved country South Africa. Secondly, our higher justice and legal system, from the High Court to the Supreme Court and Constitutional Court, must be commended and admired, proudly independent and free of political interference; whilst the lower courts at the magistrates' level, the public prosecutors and the investigation division, the Scorpions and now the Hawks are a real cause for concern as there is mounting evidence of lack of competency and dubious political appointments.

Having had this door closed in my life I decided to register at St Augustine College to further my religious studies for a degree in Theology or, more ambitiously, for a Master's degree. I felt fairly confident that I would be accepted as a student as I had practiced as a Chartered Accountant since 1964, ran a successful audit practice, completed a number of postgraduate courses in higher taxation and estate administration and was fairly involved in our parish in the community. But there was an issue as my qualifications were not considered of a standard acceptable to the university. It was suggested that I do a bridging course for one year – I think it was in communication- and, depending on the results of the year-end exams, I could again reapply for admission at the university.

It was about this time that I started to look at and think deeply about the immediate problems facing the Church and families in a hostile world. I started to research by reading books and publications and searching the internet for related information. I suppose at the back of my mind I thought that one day in the distant future this could be the subject of my thesis for my Master's degree ,as it had practical use in the everyday crisis facing the Church and the family unit. I made a decision to collate all the notes I had made over the years and collected photocopies of articles scattered all over my study in many different files. I then started to put together a book with great difficulty, using Word on my I-Pad. Looking back, it has been both stimulating and humbling to see what I have achieved with the inspiration and help of the Holy Spirit.

My book *Of Family and Faith* is a sincere attempt to help address the issues facing all of us today. Needless to say, by challenging myself and facing the realities of the world in which we live has helped me tremendously in my own journey of faith.

It is my hope that families will come to understand their important position in society and the active and meaningful role the Church must play in confronting the many challenges of today.

Some years later, out of the blue, I was contacted by Billy Davies from Trinity Church in Braamfontein, whose group of aspiring deacons were in the class behind my initial class, to join them as they were trying to arrange their ordination with Archbishop Buti Thlagale. I was invited to attend their practical training courses in 2010 and finally, I was ordained with their class as a deacon at Christ the King Cathedral on 30th April, 2011.

My role as a deacon at St Joseph's Parish in Primrose is to assist the parish priest at Mass, deliver homilies, assist with or conduct baptisms, weddings and funerals and run the RCIA courses to prepare those who wish to become Catholics or deepen their understanding of their faith, and to visit the sick.

From time to time I reflect on my decision to become a deacon and the role I play in the parish and the broader Church. I am indeed humbled by the huge responsibility I have taken on, but at the same time excited by the meaningfulness of the personal transformation in my life. God called me to service and when He decided the time was right, I was ordained a deacon – but first I had to undertake a long and arduous journey.

Only recently, when preparing for a homily, I came across an interesting explanation of what it means to be humble. At the time of my ordination, I thought it was my decision to become a deacon rather than responding to God's call.

Albert Nolan, a South African Dominican priest, is a well-known theologian, writer and speaker. He begins one of his books *Jesus Today, a Spirituality of Radical Freedom* by challenging us to think about the problems, crises and opportunities of our time. He has this to say about being humble.

He writes:

However, it is important to notice that you cannot become humble by merely deciding to do so. No amount of determination and will power can make you humble. The harder you try, the less you are likely to succeed, because this kind of effort will be the work of your ego. What you can do is become more aware of your pride or lack of humility of your ego.

Humility is a matter of truth, of recognising the truth about yourself. To imagine that you are superior to other people when you are not, or inferior to others when you are not, would be to have a false image of yourself. Recognising the truth about yourself entails recognising the futility of all comparisons in terms of superior and inferior. Competition and rivalry are the work of the ego.

Since the ego is a false image of oneself, the best way to undermine or sideline it is to grow in awareness or consciousness of the truth about oneself without comparing and without competing.

It is nevertheless truly humbling to trace my role as a deacon back to the very first deacons in the Church shortly after the death of Christ more than 2 000 years ago.

We read in Acts of the Apostles (*6:2b-5a*) about how the diaconate came about when the Apostles saw the need for men to assist in the running of the Church, as the widows and orphans had been neglected: "*It is not right for us to neglect the Word of God in order to wait on tables. Look around your own numbers, brothers, for seven men acknowledged to be deeply spiritual and prudent, and we shall appoint them to this task. This will permit us to concentrate on prayer and the ministry of the word.*"

The proposal was unanimously accepted by the community.

There is good reason to believe that St Stephen, whose feast day is celebrated on 26th December, was one of the 72 disciples chosen by Christ to go out and spread the Word. After the Ascension, he was chosen as one of the seven deacons. The ministry of the seven was very fruitful. However, many of the Jewish leaders rose in dispute with him and he was charged, like his divine Master, with blasphemy against Moses and against God. He was dragged outside the city gates and stoned to death.

I find that I am required to act as the go-between with the parish priest, the various parish committees and the parish at large to listen to issues on both sides and then find amicable and acceptable solutions. This helps to bring the issues of the real world into the life of the Church. No doubt the practical benefits of working in the business world and having to confront these challenges regularly are beneficial to the parish, which consists of people from all walks of life and with different needs and issues.

By choice, I am also responsible for maintenance, the gardens and improvements of the parish, which parishioners generally are willing to assist with when approached.

Since the Vatican II in 1964 the laity has been given a greater role to play in the affairs of the Church. In addition, the diaconate has been again called to play its rightful role in terms of its historical origins in the early Church, possibly with the realisation that the Church is facing a growing crisis with the shortage of priests and religious. This was also in response to the need to review the absolute power of the hierarchy and the structure of the Magisterium to modernise the Church and address the inroads made by other mainline religions, but more so, by the number of lapsed Catholics who seemingly find fulfillment in the countless new religions springing up all over, many of which are business and profit-driven, but are nevertheless hugely successful in attracting people through the use of social media, to which I believe the Church has not paid sufficient attention, to its detriment.

In September 2017, I attended the worldwide annual conference of deacons in Lourdes to further deepen my understanding of my faith, my role as a deacon in the parish and to ascertain the direction of the diaconate in the future, as mapped out by the Vatican. This was a year after Lynne and I attended the 50th anniversary of the diaconate in Rome, with Pope Francis scheduled to address us. This had to be cancelled as the Pope had been called on to mediate in the World Family Synod which had run into problems, as was to be expected with the many different cultures and traditions of Catholics worldwide.

At Lourdes, it was inspiring and heartening to see the incredible work deacons in many parts of the world undertake in their communities. In fact, it was simply mind-boggling to see the scope and breadth of the community work undertaken by deacons and their wives at tremendous personal sacrifice and cost. There is a truism in the saying that travel broadens the mind, so for us, travel helped us to witness firsthand what it means to do the work of God in other parts of the globe. For us, it was also a time of quiet reflection to delve deeper into many important issues of our daily lives and to truly appreciate the marvels of Creation. Otherwise, our very existence can become routine, boring, work-centred and most probably concentrated on our own little world.

But there are challenges ahead for the deacons, as expressed by the President of the International Diaconate Centre, Deacon Klaus Kiebling, when he addressed Pope Francis on the occasion of the Centre's 50th Anniversary on 4th June 2016 in the Vatican in these words:

Most Holy Father, we and I personally sincerely thank you for this opportunity to meet you today.

We, the deacons of the world, are struggling with many diverse pastoral challenges in our countries in which the traditions concerning the diaconate vary, as does the length of their history – the diaconate, therefore, has a different face and a different spirituality in each of our countries. But it is precisely these differences and this colourfulness which make the Diaconate International Centre such an inspiring place of learning for the Universal Church.

As a deacon, I consider myself an ambassador of Jesus Christ, an ambassador of our God made man, who showed solidarity upon death and beyond. I believe the incarnation of God is also the starting point of our own realisation as human beings. As ambassadors of Jesus Christ, we are called to accompany others in solidarity, through the Word as their journey toward the concretion of their humanity.

Diakonia is our mission – and that of all the Church. We gladly promise you that we will stay faithful to our diaconal mission - within the realms of our possibility and, with the strength which comes to us from Heaven even beyond in this context, there is a question which occupies our mind and which I dare to ask you because you are also animated by the vision of Universal Church:

Which is the place that you would assign to us, permanent deacons, within the Church?

Today, more than ever, we must stand up for our faith which is being eroded by governments in power the world over in the mistaken belief that we must tolerate all beliefs and must not do anything to offend any segment of the population.

As a result, there is no religious education taught in public schools for Christians yet the Moslems are allowed to practice their faith unhindered. For example, the wearing of a crucifix is not permitted yet Moslem girls are, in many parts of the world, permitted to wear a burka - an outer garment worn by some Islamic traditions to cover their bodies when in public.

Since my ordination as a deacon I have had to face the challenges of being incorporated into the clergy of the church and at the same time working in the real world. This new trend in spirituality for the Church poses two important questions as posed by James Martin SJ and Jeremy Langford in their book titled *Professions of Faith, Living and Working as a Catholic:*

Firstly, how does my faith influence my work?

Secondly, how does my work influence my faith?

This brings to light the interplay of faith and work. The connection between faith and work is nothing new, but what is coming more and more to the fore, is the recognition of a welcomed trend in spirituality of seeing how Christians experience God in their jobs, their families and in their community involvement. It is important to find God in the midst of the hustle and bustle of our daily lives and not to relegate God to Sunday worship or the few other Church connected activities we engage in during the week.

Proudly Catholic

I begin my weekly homily at St Joseph's parish with the words: *Brothers and Sisters in Christ.*

The reason for this is that we are a Christian community united in our belief in the risen Christ. I have no quarrel with members of the Communists and African Congress Party addressing each other "Comrade" or our Moslem friends beginning their prayers or greetings with the words *Praise be to Allah.*

However what is not acceptable is the intolerance shown to Christians, religions persons or minority groups by Moslems in parts of the Arab world, who feel that their spiritual leader Mohamed has been insulted and then take terrible revenge in retaliation. Christians have for centuries had to tolerate attacks on their beliefs and religious practices in countries where they are in the minority whilst the outside world simply looks on. It appears quite acceptable for Moslems to suppress freedom of religion and speech in their own countries but at the same time to expect complete freedom to practice their faith in non-Moslem countries.

It must be remembered that over the past 2 000 years we Christians have faced persecution, even death, to preserve our Christian values and beliefs. The many saints and martyrs recognised and revered by Christians is proof of their ultimate sacrifice for their faith.

We owe it to our children to uphold our faith. If we fail to pass on our Christian faith to future generations we will do grave injustice to them and God.

This is an enormous responsibility. We will have to answer to God one day.

Church Chuckle

I found this article in *The Southern Cross*, the oldest weekly newspaper in South Africa, which illustrates how each person's religious beliefs impact us in our daily lives – here in an amusing way.

A suburb was experiencing a terrible infestation of squirrels, and the local churches dealt with it in their own way.

The Presbyterian parish concluded that the squirrels were predestined to be there and they shouldn't interfere with God's will.

At the Anglican Church, the squirrels were hanging around the baptistery, so the vicar installed a waterslide on it to let the squirrels drown themselves. But the squirrels enjoyed the slide and they knew how to swim. Next week, twice as many squirrels turned up.

The Lutherans decided they could do no harm to any of God's creatures. So they trapped their squirrels and set them loose near the Anglican Church. Two weeks later, three times as many squirrels were back when the Anglicans took down their waterside.

The Catholic parish, meanwhile, decided to baptise and confirm all the squirrels. Now they only see them at Christmas and Easter!

Chapter 4
Parenting

Preparation As Parents

When I started to think about writing this book I wrote down the main headings I thought I would like to explore in greater depth and which I felt would help, in all sincerity and hopefully in some small way, my own immediate family.

Later this was expanded to include families in the parish which form part of my responsibilities and, in a moment of weakness, all families in the whole world. This was clearly over-ambitious but I am really concerned about the difficult challenges families have to face in the modern world.

I soon came to the realisation that this was such a huge subject that I couldn't even do it the slightest justice even although Lynne and I had lots of practical experience in bringing up four wonderfully well-adjusted sons in Graeme, Bruce, Kevin and Trevor. They married Monique, Annette, Gill and Debbie (who sadly died of cancer in December 2015) respectively and raised families.

We are truly blessed with 12 grandchildren living in different continents – in South Africa, Justine, Brenda and Courtney; Caitlin, Joshua, Emma and Samuel; in Solihull in the UK, Jessica and Thomas; in Lincoln Park, New Jersey USA, Leah-Marie, Nicholas and Julia.

Looking back over the years, especially the earlier years of our own marriage, Lynne and I realised how ill-prepared we were with so little proper training in bringing up children. From time to time as parents, we were overwhelmed by the magnitude of our responsibilities. And yet we managed somehow with solid family values and our faith.

I encourage all young couples to join like-minded groups of parents in their church or attend stimulating talks or courses and to read as many books as possible, but, as many young people simply don't read anymore nowadays, search on the internet on how to bring up your family. Who better to learn from than world-renowned experts sharing their knowledge and their considered findings and offering useful practical advice. One can always learn something new, particularly as family values, on which human worth depends, are disturbingly based on images of perfection marketed by the entertainment industry in Western culture.

In our day Dr Spock was in vogue but later generations discarded his findings and ideas as too radical. In fact, he later admitted that his own family situation was in shambles following his initial strict ideas of bringing up a family.

Beginning In Awe

As parents, we have huge responsibilities and challenges in helping our children to reach their full potential. We must care for and nurture the physical and spiritual growth of our children and grandchildren.

So much has been written by experts and these are important points of reference. Highly qualified medical men and women are available for medical consultation at an unfortunately increasingly high cost, with support from hospitals with the latest equipment. However, it is in the home and the communities we live in that the important life experiences which have a major impact later in the life of our children happen.

In my own life I have been very conscious of the reality of this well-known maxim from Saint Ignatius of Loyola (1491-1556), founder of the Society of Jesuits, although I only came across it in recent years:

> *Pray as if everything depended on God;*
> *Work as if everything depended on you.*

I recently read some interesting short articles in *Professions of Faith* edited by James Martins SJ and Jeremy Langford, which bring to light the interplay of faith and work in the Catholic tradition through the voices and experiences of people working in the real world: a Catholic business-person, Catholic police officer, Catholic spouse and a Catholic doctor, to name but a few. Each contributor was asked to answer the following two questions:

First, how does your faith influence your work?

Second, how does your work influence your faith?

This is what is becoming a welcome trend in spirituality – first-person reflections by working Christians on how they experience God in their jobs, with their families and in their community involvement.

One story, titled *Beginning in Awe: On Being a Catholic Parent* was written by Tom McGrath, who is an author and enjoys life in Chicago with his wife and two college-age daughters. It said a lot to me as it was revealing on how being a parent would demand a lot from one's faith, as well as do a lot for one's faith.

Here are some extracts which give some useful insights into parenting which we tend to leave aside in the midst of the hustle and bustle of daily life:

Being a parent begins in awe. And awe, which is akin to fear of the Lord, is a religious experience, one of the gifts of the Holy Spirit. Even the most jaded and cynical new parent, it seems, is not immune to the miraculous nature of birth witnessed up close. Our defences give way to awe.

Each of my daughter's births was an invitation to a new consciousness. These events confronted me with a truth I had previously overlooked or forgotten: that we are all miracles, products of life's incessant desire to bring forth more life. It was God, the Creator, pulling off yet another glorious encore. Standing so close to this miracle irrupting into the world changes everything forever.

Holding her in my arms, I realised how totally helpless she was and how dependent she would continue to be for years to come. I kept thinking, "When do I get off duty? Shouldn't there be someone else in charge? Someone who knows what they're doing? God, help!' And so, after awe, my second response to parenthood was prayer.

Awe and prayer: two great ways to energise your faith. They are both invitations to a transformed awareness. Awe lets you know that there are truths in life to be reckoned with, realities worth pay-ing attention to – like tenderness, commitment, honour, and care, plus an aching, fierce love. And I've learned that prayer has been a ready companion during every age and stage I have accompanied my children through. My struggles as a parent give me plenty to pray for, and my children's lives give me plenty to pray about.

My faith and my work as a parent are tightly interwoven. It's hard to tease out where exactly my faith feeds my family life and vice versa. When it comes to family, not much is neat and tidy. As Barbara Coloroso writes in Kids are Worth It! *"Parenting is an inefficient vocation." It's much more about mystery than mastery. But over time, certain lessons become clear. Here are a few:*

Family life regularly reveals the patterns of Jesus' life, death and resurrection.

We call it the paschal mystery. In family life this pattern of dying and rising shows itself early. We see it in the twin parental disci-plines of welcoming and letting go, which begin long before the child is born. When the desire to conceive a new life comes into focus, the couple dies to its old life and becomes willing to disrupt their lives in ways they cannot even yet imagine – all in order to take on the holy work of caring for another human being.

And we often need to die to our own traits that get in the way of being the parent we want to be. For some, this means nurturing the patience, consistency, or stability they never believed they had. For others it might include facing up to a debilitating addiction (to drugs, alcohol, work, and worry) they'd rather believe isn't hurting anyone.

Being a parent means you live in a community.

Living in a house with four adults and one bathroom means that I get up early and sometimes my day begins by praying might-ily that my turn at the facilities will come quickly. We have our chores. We have our chairs at the kitchen table. We have our times of daily prayer and our times of silence, occasionally preceded by a slammed door. And we certainly each have our annoying per-sonality traits that outsiders might find charming but don't wear so well day after day.

Each member of the family brings gifts to the table. Through our commitment to remaining a community of care over time, we create a safe, yet challenging, home base from which we can live the Gospel. We feel supported to live lives in which our faith, morals and values guide our days.

As a Catholic, I also know that my family is merely one community within many other larger communities, including our parish, our neighbourhood, society and the Church around the world. We're even part of the communion of saints who witness to a way of living and set of beliefs that give our lives meaning. On our own, it would be easier to let these values slide away. Living in a community that lives and worships and plays and prays together; I'm strengthened and emboldened to follow Jesus' way.

Being a parent cuts through your illusions.

Having kids guarantees you'll receive regular feedback you'll get nowhere else.

I flinched while watching the hilarious Steve Martin rendition of the film Bride of the Father, *especially that moment where his daughter describes her new fiancé as 'Just like Daddy, only brilliant'. Ouch!*

A friend told me her 14-year-old sternly instructed her one afternoon, "Now when we get to the mall, just pretend we don't know each other."

As a parent, I relish the opportunity to respond in kind, to let them try on their various personalities and styles, and through it all to be the precious and unique person shining through. At its best, family is the original "come-as- you-are-party".

Being a parent offers opportunities to perform the corporal and spiritual works of mercy.

When Jesus was asked who would qualify for heaven (Matthew 25:31-46), he tells them: "Those who feed the hungry, give drink to the thirsty, clothe the naked, and shelter the homeless." These are the stuff of daily family life. Parents do it all the time!

These mundane activities, along with the admonition to visit the imprisoned and bury the dead, have been combined into the seven corporal works of mercy that the Church enjoins us to practice as living signs of our faith. I remember the first time I heard this Gospel reading with the ears of a parent.

Prior to that time, I'd always thought I would have to go off to a foreign land and work in some sort of mission in order to live out these teachings. But lo and behold, that very morning I had served my older daughter yoghurt and fed a bottle to the baby. My wife and I had struggled to get them into church — appropriate clothes, and off to church we went.

During Mass, I thought about the work I do to keep a roof over our heads (and to afford enough extra to contribute to our parish's food pantry and take our turn making meals for the homeless shelter). What a joy it was to realise that my life as a parent offers me the very content Jesus pointed to as the way to eternal life. In church that morning, the readings helped me recognise these mundane activities, not as burdens and drudgery but occasions of grace.

I asked my wife, Kathleen, what element of her faith supports her work as a parent, and without a moment's hesitation she replied, "Romans 8:28 - For to those who love God, who are called according to his plan, all things work out for the good."

Parent Leadership

James Stenson works as an educational consultant specialising in family life and family-school relationships. He wrote about the role of parents in his books *Compass: A Handbook on Parent Leadership* and *Father, the Family Protector*. He says that he has found conscientious parents the world over sharing the same concerns for their children's future.

I must acknowledge the reproduction of the following material taken from his web page *www.parentleardership.com*:

I have written my books on Parent Leadership, the fruit of my many years' experience with families, so that you, a young parent, won't have to express this same regret in the future. I've have written them so that you can form a clearer idea of how other parents have lived as great leaders in family life and have succeeded with their sacred mission: to raise their children right. I want to help you form a "job description", so to speak, on how to succeed as a leader to your children.

Parents really win success with their children only in the long term. Parents succeed with their children when the youngsters grow up to become competent, responsible, considerate and generous men and women who are committed to live by principles of integrity, adults who bring honour to their parents through their conduct, conscience and character. Raising children to become adults like this is what parenthood is all about.

I watched many parents succeed this way, while others failed and their children eventually left our schools. Some parents saw their children mature into excellent men and women, often before they left high school. Others especially as they struggled through adolescence and young adulthood met with disappointment, regret and even tragedy.

These young people suffered from lack of self-confidence and self-control, substance abuse, protracted immaturity, irresponsible and self- destructive behaviour, aimlessness in life, troubles with careers or marriages or the law.

Through my countless conversations with fathers and mothers, I tried to account for the differences. I looked for patterns of family life among those people who eventually triumphed with their children. What did these successful fathers and mothers have in common? What was their compass? What did they manage to do right? And most importantly, what could parents and teachers learn from their experiences?

I offer these folios to help you learn from the experience of others and think deeply about your job as a parent. In my experience, busy parents today need to think carefully about what they're doing to raise their children well, that is, to become men and women of conscience and character. After all, parents have one chance and only one to raise their children right.

It's important for you to understand something from the outset: What I lay out for you in these portfolios is descriptive, not prescriptive. That is, I don't claim to have all the answers about family life, and I don't know anyone who does. What I'm doing here is describing the kind of thinking and action the compass of parenthood, that great parents have lived by and taught me in the course of my professional career. Take it or leave it, some or all of it, as you see fit.

Kids in Trouble

Clearly, something is seriously wrong in today's society. For some reasons, large numbers of parents around us are failing to form character in their children.

We look around in our workplaces and neighbourhoods and see young people in their 20's who are immature and irresolute, soft and irresponsible, uneasy about themselves and their futures. They may be technically skilled in some field and hold down decently paying jobs, but their personal lives and marriages are a wreck. In their conduct and attitudes, these young people seem permanently stuck in adolescence, that dangerous mixture of adult powers and childlike irresponsibility. Some are crippled or destroyed by substance abuse. But even if they remain drug-free (what a strange term!), many see their professional work as mere ego gratification or (an adolescent attitude) just drudgery endured for the sake of "spending money." Great numbers of them live as heartless narcissists, caring little or nothing about their parents or their children if they choose to have any. They retain within themselves, sometimes tragically, the flawed attitudes and habits of childhood. For some reason, they never quite grew up.

It's clear, certainly, that many young people like this were wounded by a childhood spent in dysfunctional families: drug and alcohol dependency, physical and sexual abuse, hopeless poverty.

But what is striking today, and more to our point here, is the huge percentage of seriously troubled youths from normal families. It seems that in our society the distinction between normal and dysfunctional has blurred. Or, to put it another way, some sort of subtle dysfunction is corroding large numbers of typical, middle-class homes.

We see the results of this all around us. Children today grow up in busy families where father and mother live together, life is comfortable and physically secure, and everyone enjoys the bountiful pleasures of a prosperous suburban lifestyle. Yet later on in adolescence and young adulthood, their lives are ravaged by alcohol and other drugs, grievous and ongoing marital discord, childish irresponsibility, lack of ideals or even goals in life, professional aimlessness and instability, reckless pleasure pursuit, trouble with the law, shapeless self-doubt and self-loathing, even murder and suicide.

Consider this disturbing fact: The suicide rate among young people in the United States is directly proportional to family income. It is kids from our wealthy and middle-income suburbs, not our poorest inner-city neighbourhoods, who most often take their own lives.

What is going wrong in our supposedly normal middle-class families today that could account for these problems? What is happening at home or not happening such that children grow older without growing up, that they arrive at adulthood without enough judgment and will and conscience to set their lives straight?

If we refer again to the books *Compass: A Handbook on Parent Leadership* and *Father, the Family Protector*, the author James Stenson says that the problem can be approached this way.

Normal American families seem to fall into two broad categories. One we could call the self-absorbed consumerist family; the second is the character-forming sporting adventure family.

In the self-absorbed family, parents do not set out, on purpose, to form character in their children. They treat family life like a picnic, a passive pleasure-centred experience, and their kids often meet with later trouble.

In the sporting adventure family, by contrast, parents do set out to form character, and they work at this for years. As a result, their family life becomes an ideal-driven adventure, a great sport, and their kids largely turn out well. Why is this?

Let's look at the self-absorbed family first which we'll contrast it with life in the sporting adventure family where things, it seems, are done right, where the parents direct themselves and their children with a moral compass, where character is imparted for life.

Consumerist parents are self-absorbed and unconcerned with growth in character strengths (ie: virtues), whether for themselves or their children. So they make family life mostly a steady series of pleasant diversions. Life for parents and kids centres around leisurely enjoyment, fun-filled entertainment a seamless array of sports, abundant food and drink, TV, shows, computer games, movies, music, parties, shopping.

Boredom, it seems, is the consumerist family's enemy, to be shunned at all costs. So children in families like this are kept relentlessly busy, constantly amused. The parents' rules in the house, if any, aim mainly at damage control: keeping squabbles and has-

sles to a minimum, keeping the kids out of trouble, keeping the kids from wrecking the place.

Consequently, in consumerist homes, children are steadily apprenticed through childhood as consumers, not producers. Every day, they avidly practice living as self-absorbed enjoyers and shoppers.

Not surprisingly, youngsters from such picnic-like homes see life as mostly play, a lifetime entitlement to happy amusement. The life of grown-up work (as they dimly understand it) is solely for piling up "spending money" we work in order to spend, we produce in order to consume. Who can blame them for this life-outlook? After all, this is all they experience in family life; and, as we've seen, children learn character mostly from personal example and repeated experience.

Sooner or later, of course, any picnic dwindles down into boredom; people get up and amble on to more alluring diversions.

And the same happens in the picnic-like consumerist family. Starting in their middle-school years, an appalling number of self-absorbed kids grow bored with juvenile amusements and avidly turn to novel kinds of powerfully pleasurable sensations: alcohol, drugs, the erotic and increasingly violent rock culture, vandalism, reckless driving, and recreational sex. Kids raised to see life as play will treat the automobile as a toy, and so will be prone to kill or cripple. Because their life has centred on things, they're disposed to put things ahead of people to treat people as objects, mere tools and toys for their use or amusement. Related to this, they see sex as a toy, a high-powered form of recreation, and so fall headlong into promiscuity, cohabitational "relationships", unwanted pregnancies, abortions, and disastrous marriages. This is no exaggeration. It happens literally every day.

The Consumerist Family: A Composite Picture

It's worth our while here to look more closely at the consumerist family's typical traits. What follows below is a composite picture of those unfortunate normal homes where children are poised for later trouble. That is, if you looked back to the childhood of many troubled adolescents and young adults, as described above, what traits of their family lives would you see over and over again with striking regularity?

Even with plenty of variations in detail, this is the pattern of consumerist families. Let's look at the parents first, then the children.

Parents Headed for Trouble

Consumerist parents live divided lives. They live as producers at work but consumers at home. In fact, to their children, they seem to work only in order to consume. Their home, far removed as it is from the real-life world of responsible adult achievement and ethical interpersonal dealings, is a place arrayed with entertainment gadgets, a site devoted to comfort, relaxation, and amusement. But this universe of comfortable delight is all that their children see and for children, "seeing is believing." This cocoon of pleasant escapism wholly envelopes children and shapes their sole experience with life. It becomes the ambience within which they fashion their deepest attitudes and habits, indeed their whole outlook on life: "Life is all about pleasure."

Being self-absorbed and centred mainly on the present, consumerist parents seldom think about their children's futures that is, what sort of men and women their children will grow up to become. Their time horizon stretches, at most, only a few months or a couple of years ahead. Almost never do they picture their children as grown men and women in their late 20's with job and family responsibilities of their own. When the parents do think of their kids' futures, they think in terms of career, not character. They think of what their children will do, not what they will be.

The parents seem to expect in fact, utterly take for granted that their children will naturally grow up OK as long as they're kept busily amused and shielded (more or less) from outside influences. In other words, they think that adult-level ethics, conscience, and sound judgment will just gradually form in their children in a natural and unaided way, along with the children's physical stature. When the parents think of character at all, they think it's something to be maintained in children, not formed from scratch.

The parents come down to the children's level, as indeed all parents should but (and here's the point) they stay there. By their own evident devotion to a "hassle-free" existence at home, off the job, they neglect to raise their children to grown-up levels of responsible thinking and acting. They do little to prepare the children for later life and lead them toward responsible service. Indeed, their children seem to have no concept what "adulthood" means except for what they see in movies and TV dramas. The parents seem clueless that they have a job to do, an action to take, a change to make in their children's minds, hearts, and wills: to strengthen each child's conscience and character for life.

Both parents give in readily to children's wishes and "feelings," even when they judge that this might be a mistake. Very often in family life they permit what they disapprove of. That is, they let children's pleas and whining override their parental misgivings. The parents are moved by their children's smiles, not their welfare, and so they will give in on many issues to avoid a confrontational "scene". Unwittingly, through their example of giving in, these parents teach their children to let strong desires, or even whims, routinely override judgments of conscience. So the children fail to distinguish between wants and needs; to the children, wants are needs. As a result, "feelings", not conscience, become a guide for action. (So, what happens later when the kids are tempted by the powerfully pleasurable sensations of drugs, alcohol, and promiscuous sex? What is there to hold them back?)

The father is a weak moral figure in the home. He does not teach right from wrong in a confident, purposeful way, and he does nothing to prepare his older children for their later lives outside the home, especially in moral matters. He defers "children's things" to his wife. To his kids, he appears mostly as an amiable, somewhat dull figure, even a sort of older sibling. In family life, the kids see him wrapped up entirely in his own leisure activities (like watching TV, playing sports) and minor repairs. Since they never see him work, they have no idea how he earns his living, or even what this term means. Moreover, he seldom shows much outward respect and gratitude toward his wife so she, too, seems a weak figure to the children.

Parents are minimal in the practice of religion. Though the family may attend a house of worship from time to time, even regularly, this is done as a thoughtless social routine. Family life includes little or no prayer, not before meals or at any other time. So children never witness their parents living a sense of responsibility toward God or some strong internalized ethic. "God" is just a word (sometimes an expletive), not a person, certainly not a friend. In the children's eyes, parents do not seem answerable to anyone or anything, except a relentlessly busy calendar.

   Of Family & Faith

Parents watch television indiscriminately and they allow "adult entertainment" into the home. Though they may restrict, more or less, their children's access to inappropriate material, they are driving home a powerful message: "When you're old enough, anything goes." Consequently, to the children, the right-wrong dichotomy becomes strictly a matter of age: "Whatever's wrong for kids is OK for grown-ups, so just wait till I turn 14!"

Children Headed for Trouble

At first glance most children from consumerist homes don't seem seriously troubled at all. Typically they're cheery and well-scrubbed, pleasant and smiling, often very active but only for things they enjoy. They're habituated to pleasant sensations. They like to be liked, and in fact, they expect to be liked no matter what they do. Since they're used to treating adults (including their parents) as equals, they appear naïvely lacking in respectful good manners. With some troubled exceptions here and there, they seem entirely carefree. Indeed most of them really are carefree, for now.

Children have a low tolerance for discomfort or even inconvenience. They are horrified by physical pain, however slight, or even the threat of it. They successfully plead and badger and stall their way out of unpleasant commitments and "hassles" promises and previous agreements, music lessons, homework, chores, appointments, deadlines.

Children believe that just about anything may be done for a laugh. If a prank or ridiculing remark toward someone amuses them and their peers, they blithely indulge in it no matter who gets hurt. They think their entitlement to fun must shove aside other people's rights and feelings. Indeed, the existence of other people's rights and feelings almost never enters their minds. Their outlook on life remains unchanged from infancy: "Me first!"

Children enjoy an abundance of spending money and leisure time. As a fixed habit, they overindulge in soft drinks, sweets, and junk food. They spend countless hours wholly absorbed in electronic sensations (computer games, television, the Internet) and other types of amusement. They are generally free to consume whatever they want whenever they want it, and this they do.

Kids show little or no respect for people outside the family:

guests, their parents' friends, teachers, salespeople, and the elderly. They seldom, if ever, display good manners in public. Please and thank you are missing from their speech. On birthdays or holidays, children rip through a mound of presents, but they neglect to write or call to say "thank you" to relatives and see no reason to. In some instances, children may be superficially pleasant to people (as long as this costs them nothing) but have zero concern for others' needs or interests.

Ironically, for all the parents' efforts to provide a pleasant home, the children hold little or no respect for them. The kids view their parents as "nice," and they'll admit they "like" Mom and Dad most of the time. But they simply do not esteem their parents as strong, and therefore emulable, people. When asked whom they do admire, they rattle off a long list of entertainment figures, especially comedians and rock performers.

Children know next to nothing about their parents' personal histories, and nothing at all about grandparents and forebears. So they have no sense of family history and moral continuity, that is, how they are the latest in a long line of mutually loving people who struggled, often heroically, to serve each other and stick together through good times and bad.

The children have no heroes in their lives, no real people or historical or literary figures who surpassed themselves in service to others and, by fulfilling duties, accomplished great deeds. In the absence of heroes to imitate, the kids admire and pattern themselves after coarsely freakish media "celebrities" and make-believe cartoonish figures. (As someone wise once said, "If kids have no heroes, they'll follow after clowns").

Children don't care about causing embarrassment to the family. Often they don't even understand what that might mean, for they have no framework for grasping what's shameful. They are unmoved by any cultivated sense of "family honour." If children's dress and public behaviour cause shame to the parents, that's just too bad.

Children complain and whine about situations that can't be helped: bad weather, reasonable delays, physical discomfort, moderately heavy workloads, personality differences, and the like. Their most common word of complaint is "boring".Since their lives at home are micromanaged rather than directed, they're accustomed to having their problems solved by over-solicitous grown-

ups. They've found through experience that if they hold out long enough, someone will eventually step in to make their troubles go away. Consequently, they learn to escape problems, not solve them. They learn to shun discomfort, not endure it.

Children have no serious hobbies except television watching, computer games, surfing the Web, and listening to music (mostly rhythmic noise). Their lives seem entirely plugged into electronic devices and they don't know what to do without them. Their thinking is dominated by the entertainment culture; in some senses, they believe in it. They know the words to dozens of songs and commercials, but they know nothing of the Ten Commandments.

Children (even older ones and teens) tend to form opinions by impulse and vague impressions. They are scarcely ever pressed to rely on reasons and factual evidence for their judgments. Thus they're easily swayed by flattery, emotional appeals, and peer-group pressures. They fail to recognise claptrap as in advertising, pop culture, and politics when they see it. They follow the crowd wherever it goes. They loosely sense that something is "cool," but they cannot express why.

Children never ask the question "Why?" except to defy directions from rightful authority. They are intellectually dull, even inert, showing little curiosity about life outside their family-school-playground universe. In school, moreover, they're often incorrigibly poor spellers and sloppy writers. That is, they are careless in work and do not take correction seriously. For them, nearly all enjoyment comes from escapist amusement, not from work well done, serious accomplishment, fulfillment of duty, serving others, or personal goals achieved through purposeful effort. If a task isn't "fun", they're not interested.

Children have little sense of time. Since they hardly ever have to wait for something they want, much less earn it, they have unrealistic expectations about the time needed to complete a task. They estimate either too much or too little. Consequently, large tasks are put off too long or small jobs appear mountainous. Even older children approaching high-school age have virtually no concept of deadline or of working steadily within a self-imposed time frame. The children seem to drift along in a free-floating, ever-present now and this state of mind continues well into adolescence and even young adulthood.

Throughout high school and college, they view school as one last fling at life, not a preparation for it. Graduation looms as a poignantly sad event, for they see the best part of life as behind them, not ahead. What lies ahead is trouble, the "hassles" (as they put it) of real-life work, responsible commitments, day-to-day routine, budgets and bills, two-week vacations, sharply diminished freedom, and a decline in their standard of living. So who looks forward to this? Who can endure it? Why grow up?

As explained already, this picture of a family headed for trouble is just a composite sketch, not a comprehensive description. Certainly, there are gradations among families; some families will show some of these characteristics, but not all of them. Nonetheless, over and over again, the features listed here show up in the personal histories of troubled adolescents and young adults who have come we must stress this again from an apparently normal home.

Parenting Adult Children

They are old enough to drink, vote, drive, engage in sex and marry, but you're still their parents and they need you, so how do you guide grown-up children?

I happened to page through a women's magazine *Woman and Home* on the lounge table at home and found a short article with some extremely useful tips from psychologist Sarah Newton (*Help! My Teenager is an Alien*) on how to communicate with teens, a parenting expert Jane Isay (*Walking on Eggshells*) who explores the adult child-parent relationship and a psychotherapist Gael Linderfield (*Self-Esteem Bible*) whose book advises how to gain confidence in business, relationships and social life.

I must confess that we had four sons whom we somehow managed during these difficult years and all four married in their twenties and moved out to start their own families. We often hear that daughters in the house are more challenging and need a different approach. Maybe we did something right in encouraging all four sons to go to university to study for a degree and to play active sport while staying at home and giving them one old Volkswagen Passat which was handed down between them over their years at varsity

So you've seen your children through the school years and want to encourage their independence, but how should you respond to those common problems all parents are confronted with their offspring?

Interestingly the short article by the three experts handle the issues in three parts:

The 'Just Emerging Years', 18 to 24.

Problem One: They can't seem to cope away from home.

The key is not to rush in and make everything better. This generation's 'helicopter' parents often try to micromanage everything, from matric results to choosing universities and even loitering during first-year's orientation week. Don't. Sympathise if they phone with problems, asking them what they think they can do to solve the issues they face. Independence doesn't magically happen, it takes practice.

Problem Two: They are always needing money

If you constantly bail out adult children of any age, the first message you give them is, "You're not competent to cope on your own." The second is, "It doesn't matter, because the bank of Mom and Dad will always see you through". But it is especially tempting with 18- to 22-year-olds who seem (at least to us) too young to manage. The first step is to agree in advance what you will pay for, like their phone bill. Second, is it possible for them to earn money with a student job? If they continually run out of cash, send them small amounts two or three times, but be clear (give warnings verbally, by SMS and by e-mail, so they can't plead ignorance) that the money has to last and you won't be sending any more. As long as they haven't got any mental health or addiction issues, they should be able to figure it out.

Problem Three: They can't manage their work

If your kids are really struggling, resist picking up the phone to their lecturer, and instead suggest your child arranges a meeting with the lecturer. They might fail exams or coursework initially, but motivating themselves and studying on their own are probably the most important lessons they can learn at college or university. Remember, they are always much smarter and tougher than you think.

The 'Transformation Years', 25 to 30

Problem One: They're living at home and have no direction

If they're still living with you, sit down and help them make a plan. Yes, it's very hard for young people in the job market at the moment, but any sort of job will help with confidence, self-esteem and finances.

They should find a job, even if it's part-time and not the career of their dreams. Unless they're saving for a bond or a rent deposit, work out a contribution in relation to what they earn, how much help they give around the house and, if necessary, set a moving -out date.

Problem Two: You hardly ever hear from them!

It's very tempting to phone and message when you don't hear from your children, but the best gift you can give them is having a fulfilling life of your own. A big turn-off is constantly asking for information about their lives, what they are doing, where they are. Instead, tell them about you. Make them laugh, send silly photos or a joke. Bribery works, too. Pay for their plane tickets or petroleum, if you can, invite them to share part of your holiday.

Problem Three: They are making mistakes!

However much you'd love to give them advice, the simple rule is: don't. If their home is a mess, they seem to work too much (or too little) or have a partner you don't like, pretend not to see and stay calm and polite. Similarly, what your child eats, how much they drink and what they wear have nothing to do with you. Be supportive and kind, and keep lines of communication open. Ask how they are, but don't venture an opinion on their weight or alcohol consumption. The exception is if you fear they have a mental-health or addiction problem.

The 'Getting Established Years', 35 and over

Problem One: This is tough because we all want to see our kids find love, yet it's not something we can fix for them. All you can do is to be supportive, listen and try to boost their confidence by pointing out the things that are going right and their undoubted talents. Just your presence, rock-like and stable, is enough to give them the foundations to live life confidently and fully.

Problem Two: They have found love… with the wrong person!

Unless the love of their life is abusive or seriously undermining, you just have to seek out your child's good points, and overlook the bad. If your prospective son-or- daughter's -in-law's manners aren't quite what they should be, focus on their kindness, loyalty to your child, or their stoicism in tough times. Make friends with them and take their sides. Your son or daughter will appreciate it because you are validating them and their choice, too.

Problem Three: Grandkids ……… or a lack thereof.

If your child has decided not to have kids, can't have them or hasn't met the right partner, conceal your feelings and cherish the relationship you have with your son or daughter. If a baby arrives, be an amazing grandparent, but don't offer unsolicited advice – give young parents space and tell them what an amazing job they're doing.

More Serious Problems

If you're worried your adult kids may have mental health or addiction issues, *toughlove.org.za* and *safmh.org.za* are good starting points for getting help. If they have debt issues, *payplan-solutions.co.za* and *justmoney.co.za* are geared towards helping young adults with payment plans, counselling and advice.

Hovering In The Background

Once you have children of your own, it is important to appreciate how your role must change in their lives as they grow up and lead separate lives. But as a parent you should always be somewhere in the background ready to respond with help when requested, lend a shoulder when there is pain, listening carefully to the issues and giving advice guardedly. There is nothing worse than to be in the centre of a family disagreement and be blamed for causing it or sowing seeds of discontent.

I have tried to interact separately with each of my four sons when they were growing up and later with their wives and the grandchildren according to their individual traits, strength and weaknesses. It is a mistake to treat all of them as a single group because each has a distinctive personality which needs to be recognised and nourished.

By way of illustration my son Bruce struggled to find his niche in life after leaving school. He played professional soccer for Wits University but after failing his first year in architecture, he switched to accountancy. But, failing again his first year, he was called up to do his two-year compulsory military training in the South African Defence Force. He was requested, or was it a military order, to assist his superior with his tutorials for his university studies. He found he had time then to study by correspondence for a B Com degree and afterwards served articles with a small auditing firm. After he and Annette got married he realised that with a young family he had to work hard at his studies to pass the final Board Exam to qualify as a Chartered Accountant. Just before he wrote for the third time and seeing how desperate he was to pass I gave him an inspirational poem as paternal advice to look beyond the exam but to life itself. At his 50th birthday party in 2018, I included the poem in my speech to remind the family and friends the road Bruce had travelled to achieve success in life.

IF

This poem was written by Rudyard Kipling (1885-1936)

I read that Kipling said that, in writing the poem, he was inspired by the military actions of Leander Starr Jameson, leader of the failed Jameson Raid against the Transvaal Republic to overthrow the Boer Government of Paul Kruger. The failure of that mercenary coup d'etat aggravated the political tensions between Great Britain and the Boers, which led to the Second Boer War (1899- 1902).

The words of the poem are truly inspirational. In India, a framed copy of the poem was affixed to the wall before the study desk in the cabins of the officer cadets at the National Defence Academy at Pune and the Indian Naval Academy at Ezhimala. In Britain, the third and fourth lines of the second stanza of the poem: *"If you can meet Triumph and Disaster/and treat those two impostors just the same"* is written on the wall of the players' entrance to the Centre Court at Wimbledon. These same lines appear at the West Side Tennis Club in Forest Hills, New York, where the US Open was played.

Here are the words of the poem which I like to read from time to time for inspiration to put things in proper perspective when I need a quiet inner voice to help me if I experience serious doubts or ponder on my unrealistic and impossible dreams:

> *If you can keep your head when all about you*
> *   Are losing theirs and blaming you.*
> *If you can trust yourself when all men doubt you,*
> *   But make allowance for their doubting too;*
> *If you can wait and not be tired of waiting,*
> *   Or being lied about, don't deal in lies.*
> *Or being hated, don't give way to hating.*
> *   And yet don't look too good, nor talk too wise:*
> *If you can dream- and not make dreams your master;*
> *   If you can think – and not make your thoughts your aim;*
> *If you can meet Triumph and Disaster*
> *   And treat those two imposters just the same:*
> *If you can bear to hear the truth you've spoken*
> *   Twisted by knaves to make a trap for fools,*
> *Or watch the things you gave your life be broken,*
> *   And stoop and build 'em up with worn-out tools:*
> *If you can make one heap of all your winnings*
> *   And risk it on one turn of pitch-and-toss,*
> *And lose, and start again at your beginnings*
> *   And never breathe a word about your loss;*
> *If you can force your heart and nerve and sinew*
> *   To serve your turn long after they are gone,*
> *And so hold on when there is nothing in you*
> *   Except the Will which says to them: "Hold on! "*
> *If you can talk with crowds and keep your virtue,*
> *Or walk with Kings - nor lose the common touch,*
> *   If neither foes nor loving friends can hurt you.*
> *If all men count with you, but none too much;*
> *   If you can fill each unforgiving minute*
> *With sixty second' worth of distance run,*
> *   Yours is the Earth and everything that's in it,*
> *And, which is more – you'll be a Man, my son!*

Counselling

A useful book to read is the classic *Hide and Seek* by James Dobson, which offers insightful counselling which has assisted millions of parents and teachers over the past 25 years with practical pointers for raising self-confident, healthy children. As parents, we need to be aware that investigations conducted at the University of Minnesota have found that more than half, and perhaps as much as 70 per cent, of the basic temperament of children is attributed to hereditary factors and not as a result of environmental influences. This means that children are the way they are because of the characteristics with which they are born.

It is therefore essential, indeed imperative, that parents play a significant role in developing what each child will become.

The following extracts from the book give useful insights into the subject of counselling:

The success of the parent-child relationship depends on the perceptive skill of parents to get behind the eyes of each child, seeing what the child sees, feeling what the child feels and hoping what the child hopes.

But how can this ability be attained? It is acquired by developing an understanding of the meaning of their behavior which is called "a crisis of confidence" which gnaws on the soul by day and invades the dreams at night. So then, it is suggested to understand the meaning of behaviour of our children, husband or wife, friends and even our enemies, we must begin by investigating the ways we human beings typically cope with self-doubts and personal inadequacies.

The writer then summarises the six most common ways children and adults deal with inferiority and he lists their main characteristics and discusses them in some detail.

Pattern 1: I'll withdraw.
Pattern 2: I'll fight.
Pattern 3: I'll be a clown.
Pattern 4: I'll deny reality.
Pattern 5: I'll conform.
Pattern 6: I'll compensate.

Our children are in the midst of a crisis of confidence. From the moment they enter the world, children are subjected to a value system that reserves respect and esteem for only a select few. Those who fail to measure up to society standards - primarily in areas of beauty and intelligence – must learn to cope with feelings of inadequacy and inferiority.

A new generation of parents is offered specific instruction on how to:

- Build confidence from infancy onward
- Protect children from the pain of inferiority
- Compensate for ridicule and unfair value judgements
- Teach children to respect themselves and others
- Shape the will without breaking the spirit
- Avoid overprotection and dependency
- Maximise educational potential

With the assurance that if parents succeed in imparting these values on their children then they will have the courage to SEEK their best rather than HIDE in fear.

The two reviews quoted on the back cover of this book are full of praise of the merits of this publication:

Review 1: A warm book of rare understanding with much practical material for solving family problems of insecurity.

Review 2: Dobson is specific in his advice and balances the spiritual and psychological side of the problem.

I felt it worthwhile recording the entire last chapter of the book under the heading *The Only True Values*, as it encapsulates the issues and challenges that confront parents, teachers and caring persons who want to seek solutions to help children to lead better and meaning lives.

Finally, we return to the point at which we began – with the question of human worth.

Having rejected physical attractiveness, intelligence, and materialism, as determiners of value, we must decide what will take their places. Have you consciously examined the principles you are teaching your children? Are you following a well-conceived game plan on their behalf, instilling healthy attitudes and concepts? That instructional responsibility is much too important to handle in a haphazard manner.

Without question, the most valuable contribution parents can make to children is to instill in them a genuine faith in Jesus Christ.

What greater source of confidence can there be than knowing that the Creator of the universe is acquainted with us personally; that he values us more than the possessions of the entire world; that He understands our fears and anxieties and reaches out to in immeasurable love when no one else cares; that He turns our liabilities into assets and our emptiness into fullness; that He sent His only Son to die for us and has promised us life, where handicaps and inadequacies will be eliminated and pain, suffering and tears will no more than dim memories.

What a beautiful philosophy with which to "clothe" a child! What a wonderful message of hope and encouragement for the depressed teenager who feels crushed by life's circumstances. This is self-worth at its richest, not dependent on the whims of birth or social judgement or the cult of the super child, but on divine decree. If this be "the opiate of the people" as Karl Marx sneered, then I have staked my entire life on the validity of its promise.

Not only is Jesus Christ the source of all meaning in life, but He is the only one who can free us from the tyranny of the self. Christian principles place the spot-light on others rather than on ourselves, while granting human worth on a completely different scale of values than society does. The Master never told us that the beautiful people have an inside track. He never granted special favours to intellectuals. He is not partial to the wealthy. He is unimpressed by blue-blood heritage. In fact, He expressed disdain for such values in Luke 16:25 : For what is highly esteemed among man is an abomination in the sight of God. In other words, God actually hates the things that we value most highly, because He sees the folly of our worshipping that which can be kept for such a brief time.

But what does God value? We cannot substitute His system for ours unless we know what He has personally ordained. Fortunately, the Bible provides the key to his value system for mankind. It seems to be composed of seven all-important principles:

- *Devotion to God;*
- *Love for others;*
- *Respect for authority*
- *Obedience to divine commandments;*
- *Self-discipline and self-control;*

- *Humbleness of spirit, and*
- *Repentance and forgiveness through a personal relationship with Jesus Christ.*

These seven concepts are from the hand of the Creator, and they are absolutely valid and relevant for today. When applied to life, they encourage a child to SEEK out opportunities rather than HIDE in lonely isolation. They lead not to despair, as do humanistic values, but to emotional and physical health. Isn't this what Isaiah meant when he wrote: And all thy children shall be taught of the Lord; and great shall be the peace of thy children (Is 54:13).

The healthy self-concept Christ taught involves neither haughtiness nor self-loathing. It is one of humble reverence for God and every member of the human family. We are to see our fellow human beings as neither better nor worse than ourselves. Rather, we are to love them as ourselves, and that prescription puts the entire matter of self-worth into its proper perspective.

Children need to look up with pride to their parents who are their primary role models.

Parents who fail in this regard are heaping untold misery and grief on their children and on themselves.

Elements of Counselling

Recognising just how important it is to be able to talk about ourselves to ourselves and to each other, this excellent publication *Elements of Counselling - A Practitioner Handbook* by Joan Schon, Lauren Gower and Victor Kotze underlines the value of knowing how to listen and when to speak.

This hands-on guide to short-term counselling is for everyone from doctors and nurses to pastors and teachers, and neighbours, friends and families.

The book is about the importance of being able to talk about and share difficult emotions with each other and to face them in ourselves. It is about understanding when to talk, what to say, and most importantly, about how to listen.

When we counsel people we want our work to be therapeutic, to bring relief and to convey our empathy and understanding to our clients (and family members who are need not knowing of our help).

This accessible publication achieves the goal of building capacity without being simplistic, by providing an understanding of psychoanalytic things and its application to counselling. It functions like the biblical analogy 'give a person a fish and you feed them for one day; give a person a fishing rod and you feed them for life'.

Chapter 5
Family Values

Nothing Has Really Changed For Mankind

The inscription on a tablet from Constantinople 3800 BC.

We have fallen upon evil times, and the world has waxed

very old and wicked;

Politics are very corrupt;

Children are no longer respectful to their parents.

These words are equally applicable to our world of the 20th century.

The Breakdown of Family Life

The biggest challenge facing the world today must be without any doubt the major breakdown of the modern family life.

To start with, we are all are one way or another the product of our being members of a unique unit comprising of a husband and wife united in love, certainly at the start of the relationship. Marriage is a give-and-take, life-long commitment needing constantly attention by both husband and wife. It is a love story that began at creation with God's steadfast love for His people, which required a response to that love from a man and a woman.

Marriage

The United Nations has defined marriage *as a union between two persons.* Note the specific emphasis of the words *as a union between a a man and a woman.*

This pronouncement is no doubt in response to the present liberal sentiments sweeping across the world like wildfire. It is part of the pendulum of the clock swinging too far to the left, which has a dramatic effect on how religion and marriage are viewed in a world too easily swayed by popular practices and opinions. Sadly, religious leaders, politicians and the public have not looked ahead to try and assess how this will dramatically change our future. Without a doubt there will be serious consequences and hurdles to overcome socially, economically and politically, impacting the very fabric of families and society.

The modern world has sadly, in many instances, tended to view marriage as a form of mere emotional satisfaction that can be constructed in any way or modified at will. But the indefensible contribution of marriage to society transcends the feelings and momentary needs of the couple. As the French bishops have taught, it is not born *'of loving sentiment, ephemeral by definition, but from the depth of the obligation assumed by the spouses who accept to enter a total communion of life'*.

Even though my wife Lynne and I have been happily married for 52 years we are still mere novices in this lifelong commitment to each other. We are still learning what marriage is all about and frankly, we accept we will never completely appreciate or begin to master all that needs to know about this unique relationship in our own lifetime.

Nevertheless, having made this obvious admission of my own inadequacy, I still feel compelled to try to explain the Christian belief, even with my own limited knowledge and practical experience and personal beliefs on marriage, as otherwise, this book which seeks to promote family and faith would be of little or limited value.

What follows on the subject of marriage has been taken from the different Catholic Bishops Conferences held all over the world which explain the Christian position far better than I could ever hope to do. However be warned that I have only scratched the surface, but there is enough here to help in the understanding of this fundamental cell of society under serious threat in today's world.

Married love is a unique form of love between a man and woman which has a special benefit for the whole of society, as concluded by *Relatio Synodi* of the Third Extraordinary Assembly of the Synod of Bishops (5-19 October 2014). The Catholic Church, with other Christian Faiths and those of no particular religious view, regard the family, based on marriage between a woman and a man, as the single most important institution in any society.

To seek to re-define the nature of marriage would be to undermine it as the fundamental building block of our society. The Church seeks with others to reaffirm the rational basis for holding that marriage should be reserved for the unique and complementary relationship between a woman and a man from which the generation and upbringing of children are uniquely possible.

This understanding of marriage is deeply rooted in all cultures: it is not intended to exclude or disadvantage anyone.

God's plan for marriage, according to the Book of Genesis, shows us that man and woman are created in the image and likeness of God; they recognise that they are made for each other (*Gen 1:24-31; 2:4b-25*). Through procreation, man and woman collaborate with God in accepting and transmitting life: '*By transmitting human life to their descendants, man and woman as spouses and parents co-operate in a unique way in the Creator's work*' (*Catechism of the Catholic Church No 372*).

Jesus himself teaches that marriage is between a man and a woman: "*Have you not read that from the beginning the Creator made them male and female. For this reason a man shall leave his father and mother and be joined to his wife, and the two shall become one flesh*" (*Mt 19: 4-6*).

As Christians, our primary Commandment is to love. Love always demands that we respect the dignity of every person. That is why the Catholic Church clearly teaches that people who are homosexual must always be treated with sensitivity, compassion and respect. It is not lacking in sensitivity or respect for people who are lesbian, gay, bisexual or transgender but points out that same-sex relationships are fundamentally and objectively different from opposite-sex relationships and that society values the complementary roles of mothers and fathers in the generation and upbringing of children.

The meaning of marriage is that it is a unique relationship different from all others.

An essential characteristic of marriage is the biological fact that a man and a woman can join together as male and female in a union that is orientated towards the generation of new life. The union of marriage provides for the continuation of the human race and the development of human society.

It is precisely the difference between man and woman that makes possible this unique communion of persons, the unique partnership of life and love which is marriage.

Male-female complementarity is intrinsic to marriage. It is naturally ordered toward sexual union in a faithful, committed relationship as the basis for the generation of new life. The true nature of marriage, lived in openness to life, bears witness about how precious is the gift of a child is and to the unique roles of a mother and father.

A man and woman united in marriage, as husband and wife, witness to God's plan for both life and love in a way that no other relationship of human persons can.

Marriage is not merely a private institution. The well-being of the family and its place in society is not simply a matter for the husband and wife but for society as a whole. It is given special recognition by society because it is the place where children learn what it means to be members of their family and of society.

Marriage is important because in marriage, a woman and man promise love and fidelity to each other, for the rest of their lives. Not knowing what lies ahead, they nevertheless make a commitment that they will continue to love each other whatever comes. While we know that their commitment may break down and know also the sorrow that this can bring, we also recognise that many couples live that marital commitment faithfully.

This committed, married love provides a stable and nurturing environment for children. It is here that children receive the most important and lasting education of all. They learn how to be a member of a family and of society.

Society recognises the many challenges that married couples have to face today in building and sustaining a strong marriage.

A major challenge arises from any proposal which seeks to redefine the meaning and purpose of marriage on which the family is founded, changing the definition of marriage by enabling the relationship of a same-sex couple also to become a marriage. To do this would mean that marriage, under civil law, would no longer be the committed gift of a man and a woman in a relationship until death do us part, in the kind of union which can bear fruit in the form of new human lives. Any such proposal is based on the assumption that the institution of marriage on which the family is founded, which has always been recognised as the natural, primary and fundamental unit in society, has nothing unique about it and on the assumption that marriage can be stripped of that social standing without obscuring its irreplaceable social role.

It is a matter of justice to protect the union between a man and a woman. A husband is a man; a wife is a woman who has a husband. A same-sex couple cannot be husband and wife. A same-sex couple cannot procreate a child through the sexual act which expresses married love.

Often those who call for legal recognition of same-sex marriage see it as a matter of fairness, equality and civil rights. The Church holds that basic human rights must be afforded to all people. This can and should be done without sacrificing the institution of marriage and family and the fundamental role they play in society. This is not about denying civil rights but protecting and upholding the meaning of marriage.

It is a grave injustice if the State ignores the uniqueness of the role of husbands and wives, the importance of mothers and fathers in our society. Children, as they grow and mature, deserve from society a clear understanding of the importance of marriage. Without protection and support for this unique place of marriage in society, the State could, in effect, deprive children of the right to a mother and father.

Religious and non-religious people alike have long acknowledged and know from their experience that the family, based on the marriage of a woman and a man, is the best and most ideal place for children. It is a fundamental building block of society which makes a unique and irreplaceable contribution to the common good. It is therefore deserving of special recognition and promotion by the State.

Proposals to change the meaning of marriage effectively say to parents, children and society that the State should not, and will not, promote any normative or ideal family environment for raising children. It, therefore, implies that the biological bond and natural ties between a child and its mother and father have no intrinsic value for the child or for society.

Pope Francis said this in his address to members of the International Catholic Child Bureau at an audience in the Vatican on 16 April 2014: *"We must reaffirm the right of children to grow up with a father and a mother capable of creating a suitable environment for the child's development and emotional maturity."*

There will always be situations in which the best interests of a particular child can only be met in a different type of arrangement. It is important that the State provides for and gives practical support to these arrangements. This is different, however, from saying that having children raised by their biological parents in a life-long committed marriage is no longer essential to the common good and deserving of special recognition by the State. Even where a husband and wife cannot have children of their own, the nature of their marriage can still provide a mother and a father to a child in adoption or fostering. We believe that the State should urgently provide more and better services in support of marriage in which mothers and fathers can provide the optimum loving and stable environment for children to grow and flourish

Marriage as a Sacrament requires total communion of life and of love with God of the married couple in their family life.

The love of husband and wife is recognised as a foundational society reality in societies and religions in every part of the world was acknowledged by *Relatio Synodi* of the Third Extraordinary Assembly of the Synod of Bishops (5-19 October 2014) when it was recorded:

Acknowledging *and affirming the respect due to the institution of marriage, the Catholic understanding of marriage adds a new 'dimension'; it is a special blessing from Christ.*

Marriage is a sacrament, a sign of God's love. It mirrors the love of Christ for his Church. Marriage is a total communion of life and of love with God of the married couple in their family life.

Through the help of the grace of the Sacrament, God consecrates the love of husband and wife and confirms the indissoluble character of their love, offering them assistance to live their faithfulness, mutual complementarity and openness to new life.

It is the vocation and mission of married couples to be a visible sign of God's love, to one another, to their children and to the community through a faithful relationship when is open to life.

The love of God is eternally faithful and reliable. Married love seeks to reflect that love as a faithful, unbreakable relationship. Because it is a sacrament, marriage brings about and deepens the love it reflects. With the couple living in the sacrament of marriage, their children are enriched by their sharing in God's love.

It is rightly said that marriage and the family are under great pressure today. There are economic pressures, worries about health, the pain of unemployment and emigration, and the social pressures, especially on younger members. Every family has its problems.

But instead of beginning with the problems and challenges, we might begin by reflecting on the meaning of marriage as a sacrament and the blessing that it can be to the couple and to society.

Christians have always known marriage is not easy. As the marriage begins, in the marriage ceremony, the bride and groom promise to be true to one another 'for better, for worse, for richer, for poorer, in sickness and in health'. The love of Christ for us, which marriage reflects, led him to betrayal, abandonment by friends and agonising death on a cross. But that was also the path that led him and leads us to the fulfillment where 'Death will be no more; mourning and crying and pain will be no more' (Rev 21:4) and where God will make all things new. In this uncertain world, with all its pain, Christian marriage is lived in the promise of the 'great hope which can only be God' as expounded by Pope Benedict XVI in his Encyclical letter *Spe Salvi* (2007).

Faith in Christ, lived in the sacrament of marriage, opens for the couple the truth that gives life meaning, the hope which can make sense when they face difficult challenges and poverty and sickness together.

Women and men find companionship in that relationship, where they complement each other, not because they are the same but because they are different, with the different interests, perspectives, experiences and family backgrounds that each of them brings to the relationship. They are different because of all these things, but they are different also because they are of different sexes. The difference means for most couples that their relationship can be fruitful in a unique way. Their love can bring forth new human life. In the child of their love, they will see the qualities and experiences that each of them has, flowering in a new human being. This little person is a member, like them, of the human family and, like them, a child of God who is beginning the journey that leads to where God makes all things new.

Their marriage is not just for themselves or for their children they may have. The family is the Church in the Home. The bride and groom are consecrated, and as a married couple living their vocation, they enrich the whole community, building up the Church with their love as husband and wife. In procreating and rearing children, they live the beauty of love, fatherhood and motherhood and they have the dignity of participating in God's creative work. The 'true love between husband and wife' implies a mutual gift of self and includes and integrates the sexual and effective aspects, according to the divine plan as explained by Pope Paul VI in the Pastoral Constitution on the Church in the Modern World, *Gaudium et Spes* (1965) , 48-49.

Marriage is lived in the concrete demands of everyday life as expressed in the Apostolic Exhortation, *Familiaris Consortio* (On the Role of the Christian Family in the Modern World 1982, 51) by Pope John Paul II.

As Catholics, it is not sufficient for us just to talk about the importance of family. We also have a responsibility to do all that we can do to offer practical support for marriage and families in our parish communities, in our liturgies and our pastoral action and as individual members of society, through our social and po-litical actions.

This prayer from *The Family Prayer Book* was inspired by Pope John Paul II in his Apostolic Exhortation, *Familiaris Consortio*.

God's Plan for Our Marriage and Family

> *As we answer God's call*
> *In our vocation*
> *In the Sacrament of Marriage*
> *To follow Christ and to serve*

> *The kingdom of God in our married life,*
> *we ask, in and through the concreteness of*
> *events, problems, difficulties and circumstances*
> *of everyday life*
> *that God will come to us,*
> *guiding us and enlightening us as we share*
> *Christ's love with one another, in our family life,*
> *at work, in our neighbourhood,*
> *in our contributions to society*
> *and in the life and worship of our parish.*

There is a glimmer of hope in the future for allowing divorced and remarried Catholics to receive the Eucharist, as it is possible that the initiative of the German bishops to have the Extraordinary Synod on the Family in October 2019 look in a pastorally constructive way at an issue facing the whole Church. Most families know how complex, unwished-for and painful a marriage break-up is. No one chooses it, but they have to deal with its consequences. And so should the Church, say the German bishops and any pastor with a heart. In a sincere effort to heal the pain of divorce, they are looking at the internal forum as defined in Canon 130 of the Code of Canon Law. This Canon allows for an internal forum to resolve issues that do not fit the formal judicial requirements that the Church's marriage courts require and focuses on the God-given gift of conscience. It is hoped to set up a process involving a pastor and parishioners where the reality of failure and the contributions to failure made by sinful people are recognized and forgiven. These new developments were reported in *unanews.com* by the executive director Fr Michael Kelly.

Love

This love in marriage is very special, a beautiful experience – probably the most wonderful thing that has happened in a couple's life. Deep down there must be an acknowledgement that anything so good must come from God, and you would be in the right as Joseph M Champlin explains in his book *Together for Life*.

A beautiful explanation of love was written by St Paul in 1 Cor 13:4-8 and it is rightly a popular choice of couples as one of the readings at their marriage ceremony. It is a useful reference point to reflect on when the marriage enters turbulent waters, which must happen from time to time in most marriages.

This passage stands as one of the most famous chapters of the Bible. Living a life of love marked by these qualities is a way that pleases God and brings peace, happiness and joy in the home.

> *Love is patient,*
> *Love is kind,*
> *It does not envy,*
> *It does not boast,*
> *It is not proud,*
> *It doesn't dishonour others,*
> *It is not self-seeking,*
> *It is not easily angered, it keeps no records of wrongs.*
> *Love does not delight in evil*
> *but rejoices with the truth.*
> *It always protects, always trusts,*
> *always hopes, always perseveres.*
> *Love never fails.*
> *But where there are prophecies,*
> *they will cease;*
> *Where there are tongues,*
> *they will be stilled;*
> *Where there is knowledge,*
> *it will pass away.*

Love has to be the supreme and distinguishing characteristic for all Christian. Love is all-important. Simple acts of love, performed without fanfare or publicity, are the sign that self- concern has been overcome by concern for others.

If you can't do great things, do little things with great love. If you can't do them with great love, do them with a little love. If you can't do them with a little love, do them anyway.

These words were penned by the American writer Napoleon Hill (1883 -1970).

Birth Control

Few today argue against responsible family planning. It has come to be an accepted value in our culture, endorsed as such by most concerned people and religious bodies. To say that a married couple should attempt to have only as many children as they can adequately care for is to respect a self-evident norm, a norm that most would agree with completely.

The legal freedom of individuals to use contraceptives has been recognised by most governments. In fact, in many African countries contraceptives are freely distributed in schools in an effort to prevent Aids which is a scourge of their societies. There are many social issues not properly addressed by leaders and communities, but the need to promote morality seems not to be sufficiently addressed so the elimination of Aids/HIV will be with us for the foreseeable future. The much-publicised rape case of President Zuma is an illustrative example of the problem.

The recognition of such individual freedom of action does not, by itself, make such actions either right or wrong. Obviously, there are sharply differing judgements taught by different religions, for example, the Roman Catholic Church used to forbid the use of artificial contraceptives on the grounds that human persons are no more the arbiters of the process by which human life comes to be than they are of human life already begun. Today the Church is silent on this issue so it seems acceptable for the husband and wife to decide responsively to use contraceptive methods to plan their family, although the Church promotes the concept of Natural Family Planning which helps a couple to know when her fertile and non-fertile times of the month are.

Abortion

This is without a doubt a major issue in our world today due to population explosion, religious beliefs and health issues. Abortion is the ending of a pregnancy by removal or expulsion of an embryo or fetus before it can survive outside the uterus of a woman.

Far be it for me to try and write about abortion so what follows is a collection of articles which I have read and included in this book for the sake of completeness and general information.

The past several years, a tremendous push for more permissive abortion laws has occurred in the USA and Canada. With few exceptions, the major newspapers and magazines of our countries have participated in this movement by publicizing every new de-

velopment and every argument, valid or not, in favour of more permissive abortion laws.

Those whose deep-felt convictions are pro-life have been labelled anti-abortion and have been dismissed as religionists and often, by inference, either Roman Catholic or influenced by the Church's teaching.

Population explosion, illegal abortions and their fancied toll on maternal lives, the pitiable rape or incest victim, the deformed baby, the mother's physical and mental health - these all, in turn, have been given top billing for reasons to change.

The movement has been sweeping away all who disagree. The pro-abortionists, who were setting as their highest goal the incorporation into laws of the controversial provisions of the American Law Institute's suggested changes, have now discarded that step-on-the-way and have been openly espousing nothing less that abortion-on-demand.

Theological considerations are critical to each person individually but cannot be imposed upon non-believers in the culture. This is not to minimize religious conviction. The value, dignity and right to life of each individual which has been a hallmark of and lies at the core of western culture, is at least, directly treated to our Judeo-Christian heritage.

More and more it has become evident that a consistency is noted in the Western world among those who favour abortion. This group begins with a basic social premise that a woman must have this right. This is the sine-qua-non of the pro-abortion movement. For them, it is basic and beyond challenge, much as a believing Christian starts from Jesus Christ is God.

Assuming the above to be an absolute unchallengeable need, the pro-abortionist must then justify this position. Since the idea of killing humans remains repugnant to most people, this idea has to be denied; therefore, the cornerstone of their argument has been the denial of the humanity of the being who is killed by abortion. This has partly been accomplished by the semantic gymnastics of words such as "terminate" and "interrupt" pregnancy so that the more accurate biological term "kill" can be avoided. The major ploy, however, has been to dehumanize the developing living human in the womb. It is easier to destroy a "foetus", an "embryo" or *a "product of conception" than to destroy an unborn "baby".*

If in fact, the being killed by abortion is not a human life, then, however violent the solution, however damaging it may be to the woman, there is some logic and at times, even seeming compassion to abortion.

If however, the being killed is a human life, a tiny, tiny boy or girl, then every citizen in every nation should be deeply concerned. Then, a bit of study will show the logic and reasons for the destruction of these weakest, least conscious, smallest and most innocent humans among us by abortion, can be applied just as logically and legally to the weak, only partly conscious, oldest and most dependent or defective among us by euthanasia. Then truly this is shown to be a civil rights issue of the gravest import.

Here are some practical solutions what can be done:

1. Pray

As if this were the only thing that matters, for in truth perhaps it is. Pray that God would allow our people to come to their senses (and to their knees) before we destroy ourselves.

2. Educate

Yourself and others. Speak to others, discuss, and give other literature.

3. Work

For the service groups (Birthright) the educational groups (Right to Life), the political groups (Political Action Group). Work in any and all of the ways needed, for the unborn, the aged, the unfortunate. It is only through the continuing gift our love in helping others that we will win over those who have turned to the violence of utilitarian killing to seek their ends.

4. Contribute

Time and effort and money to this effort. The pro-life effort is characterised by the heroic efforts of its volunteers and by the fact that none of the groups ever have money, they merely exist from less debt to more debt. Your stewardship is needed.

5. Vote in elections as it will be through this process that the wish of the people will be translated into electing representatives whose convictions are either pro-life or anti-life. It will only be through this process that laws and constitutional amendments can be passed that will again protect and value all human life.

6. Write

Who to? Members of parliament, newspapers, TV stations, support marches and health departments.

Here is a wonderful quotation from Albert Schweitzer to help you to realise and make up your mind of the seriousness of abortion:

If a man loses reverence
for any part of life
he will lose his reverence
for all of life.

Divorce

During a recent weekday homily at Mass at our parish priest told us that he was once approached to conduct a wedding service. He asked the couple for the date of the wedding and then he jokingly asked if the date of the divorce had been agreed upon. The couple was taken aback and looked surprised.

The couple were divorced within the first year as the husband was abusive and jealous to such an extent that the wife had to flee their home and file for a divorce. So in this day and age this could be a reasonable question to ask when it is fairly obvious that the couple are unsuitable for each other, or are ill-prepared or not serious in their commitment to each other or to the marriage, or are immature, or are marrying for the wrong reasons, or had not attended a marriage preparation course to prepare them for this serious step in their lives.

Not knowing the true situation in the world today I Googled divorce and read some very interesting facts. And, as an added bonus, I was able to access good advice, which I pass on so that couples are better informed before they enter marriage, of what to watch out for. Successful marriages require regular attention and maintenance just like your car needs servicing, change of oil and new spark plugs!

Recently members of our pub club which has met monthly for lunch for many, many years as old friends - Sue and Pat Ryan, June and Malcolm Robinson, Janet and Johnny Stanbury, Noreen and Mike Davies and Lynne and myself, talked about marriage. To start off Mike asked each couple how long they had been married, which he then added up. If I remember correctly, the total was about 250 years. Not all the couples could remember the date of their marriage so it took a little time to calculate the year! Needless to say, the wives were better than the husbands about remembering the day, month and year! In today's world, this is quite a staggering total and achievement.

We then tried to analyse why our marriages had lasted so long. Amid all the funny anecdotes, family stories and much laughter, we did manage to find some common ground about why our marriages were successful – these included serious commitment, common interests, starting off with very little worldly wealth, allowing each other space to pursue his or her own interests, practicing faith, respecting each other, strong family values in the home and doing things together as a family.

What was interesting was that we all came from stable homes with strong family ties. Our parents also experienced problems in their marriages but they seemed to overcome their troubles by communication, sticking it out and not making rash decisions. They recognised that their world faced different challenges like two World Wars, high global unemployment following the wars, fewer distractions like TV and modern social media, strong family unity and fundamental respect for each other and a belief in God.

Divorce in the family causes severe stress at the time and continues to be a thorny issue to our close-knit families with high expectations for the happiness and welfare of our children, it was sad therefore to note the number of divorces in our families. Of the 12 children, there have been four divorces - 33 1/3 %. Looking back with hindsight over the years we realise that as parents we needed to recognise the danger signs at the start of the courtship and, in some way or other, play a more active and positive role in helping our children to make a success of their marriage. Much easier said than done, as generally parents are pushed aside, especially in the earlier years of the marriage as couples rightly try and establish themselves as a new family unit.

The current statistics world-wide are depressing for couples who hope to live happily ever after. South Africa may have some way to go to match the USA, where for every 100 new marriages there are 38 divorces. By contrast, married couples in South Africa calling it quits are on the rise with the number of civil divorces increasing by 20.4% from a low of 20 980 in 2011 to 25 260 in 2015.

It is also disturbing to read that couples dreaming of a life of marital bliss are becoming a rarer breed. There was a 26% fall in new civil marriages from a peak of 186 522 in 2008 to 138 627 in 2015. At this pace, the number of civil marriages will fall below 100 000 within six years. For a variety of reasons, couples today prefer to shack up together and not to marry. This is a very sad feature of the modern world and a sure recipe for a rocky future relationship as it creates many social and legal problems for the couple. Customary marriages have also nosedived, falling from a peak of 20 259 in 2007 to 3 467 in 2 015.

Reasons for divorce are many and varied but the most common are financial and adultery - the advent of social media has made it hard to have a fling and get away with it. In this age of instant gratification, many people are no longer prepared to take the time and commitment to try and sort their problems out.

These sobering statistics might discourage married or engaged couples who are striving to beat the odds, but it's entirely possible to sustain a committed, fulfilled and intimate union that doesn't succumb to the agonising reality of divorce, which has a huge adverse impact especially on the children of the marriage.

Understanding the risk factors then working together with each other to counteract them, can help you divorce-proof your relationship and strengthen the bonds of marriage.

There are six surprising statistics about divorce, according to Maile Timon who is a blogger and content editor. She writes articles on lifestyle and family, health and fitness, education, business, how-to and more. When she is not writing, she enjoys hiking in Southern California.

So let us see what Maile has to say as it will be beneficial to take note of the pitfalls that contribute to an unsuccessful marriage. These are offered to provide more insight so that married couples can be proactive to ensure longevity and contentment in their marriage:

One is that divorce is most common during the early years. An estimated 80% of couples are headed in the direction of divorce within the first four to five years of their marriage. This startling, however common, trajectory is often because of decreased passion as excitement in the relationship wanes. As issues like finances, work and family jockey for attention, maintaining the 'spark' experienced while dating can diminish in record time. Avoid this pattern during those first critical years of marriage by prioritising emotional connection and physical chemistry on a regular basis.

Secondly, mental health issues often complicate marriage. According to Science in Health Aging and Healthcare, *if one or both partners struggle with depression, substance abuse or certain phobias, the risk of divorce often increases exponentially. This does not mean all marriages with a track-record of mental illness are destined for a courtroom settlement, but it's worth noting the heightened challenges you may encounter if either spouse is suffering. Consider professional therapy to restabilise the marriage, communicate about the issue and learn to support each other's needs.*

Thirdly, the education levels can impact your risk of divorce. Academics can play into the success of a marriage. Based on divorce research, if you've earned a Bachelor's degree, you have a better likelihood of a long-lasting marriage and spouses who both have a Bachelor's degree are 10% less prone to divorce than spouses without a college education. When each partner has the same academic level there's an increased sense of equality in the relationship. Not to mention, you both equipped to contribute more income toward the household expenses, which can safeguard your marriage from financial stresses.

Fourthly, having children is not always a marriage solution. Among the most pervasive misconceptions is that a struggling marriage can restore itself once kids enter the equation. Approximately 50% of children in North America will experience parental divorce before age 18. While the mantra of staying together for the kids' sake often prompt spouses to work through relationship issues, the assumption that child-rearing is a proven antidote for marital tensions can lead to more discontent in the future, undermining not just your partnership, but the whole family.

Fifthly, your parents' marital status has a major influence. If divorce is present within either spouse's family of origin, their own chances of marriage instability, or even separation, will often double. This occurs because the individual was raised absorbing a message that commitment and unification are not sustainable over the long-term, which gives them a defeatist attitude when problems arise. While this cross-generational pattern of divorce can strain your marriage, it's not doomed to failure. Break the cycle with trust, communication and resilience when your instinct is to quit.

Sixthly, sexual initiation can become a divorce catalyst. Engaging in intercourse with multiple partners before marriage or becoming sexually active under the age of 18 can escalate the risk of divorce within the first 10 years of marriage, according to the University of Iowa.

This research suggests that promiscuous behaviour as a young person is detrimental to the vitality of a marriage, but it's often unrealistic that both partners will enter the union without a sexual past. So remember that prior experiences don't need to dictate the health and frequency of intercourse in a marriage context. The problems arise when past promiscuity causes trust issues in a marriage. Someone's sexual past doesn't necessarily foreshadow his or her future, but that may not stop the other person's insecurity or lack of trust. Make a decision to love by trying to let go of the past and stop obsessing about the situation which broke the trust between you and your spouse.

If trust issues persist, seek professional help. You need to work through these issues, or insecurity will perpetuate the issue and lead to paranoid, clingy behaviour. In these situations, it's important to be as honest and open with one another as possible. If it means letting the other person check your cell phone or email that may be just what you need to do to build trust. This may make you uncomfortable, but it's a necessary step if you want to make your relationship last.

Your relationship is worth protecting and fighting for, even in the midst of a culture which normalises separation, divorce and broken family units. Knowing the statistics and how to avoid their repercussions could mean the difference between successful marriages that grow stronger through the years, versus an unstable marriage that doesn't stand the test of time. Just keep in mind: the odds exist, but they are beatable.

     Of Family & Faith

In closing this section it is instructive to note what attorneys have to say as they have experience in the trends of the reasons for filing for divorce. One attorney notes that the reasons for divorce are many and varied, but a number stand out, in particular, financial problems. Another attorney puts another slant on it in pointing out that in this age of instant gratification, many people are no longer prepared to take time to try and sort their problems out. There is a saying that goes around legal circles that marriage is about love and divorce is about money.

In the actual process of divorce in-court battles are something of a rarity, as all but 10% of divorces are settled out of court. But it can be a touch and go affair, as one attorney noted: *it is fair to say most divorces are settled on the steps of the court*. On the issue of divorce costs, it is very much a case of asking: how long is a piece of string? An uncontested divorce costs between R3 000 and R5 000 but it can be extremely costly if the action ends in the Supreme Court where advocates come into the picture.

Annulment of Marriage

According to John T Catoir in his book *The Dilemma of Divorced Catholics* a vast number of people are wounded by the trials of modern life which in turn is reflected in the soaring divorce rate as a result of the strains and stresses of married life. He writes:

Marriage is an indissoluble. That is the teaching of the Catholic Church. Couples who divorce must go through a civil court to obtain the order of divorce.

No one questions that marriage is indissoluble and that a truly valid marriage bond cannot be broken or dissolved, and that no one can validly begin a new marriage while an existing valid marriage is still in force. But we can and must ask questions if a serious doubt exists concerning the validity of a specific marriage in the eyes of the Church.

The Church has recognised that divorces are a reality and has set up mechanisms such as Marriage Tribunals to assist those who are experiencing the pain of a broken marriage. The question before every Church tribunal is this: Which of the marriages presented are truly valid, and which are not?

Sometimes people cannot get an annulment even after trying for years. Many of them, believing they have sound reasons for

*doubting the validity of the marriage in question, end up follow-
ing their consciences and marrying again, outside the Church.*

*St Paul's pastoral statement to the Galatians 6:2 puts the whole
issue in perspective: help carry one another's burdens, in a way
you will fulfill the law of Jesus Christ. Ever since I read that line, I
have understood clearly that the defence of all our legal principles
must be done within the supreme law of charity.*

St. Augustine said, *Do what you can do, and pray for what you
cannot do.* Many good people have followed St. Augustine's advice.

When a marriage ends in divorce there is often a sense of personal failure what was going to be so wonderful and blessed and
happy becomes instead a terrible disappointment and a living
hell. Love turns to hatred, dreams become nightmares. Confident, competent, loving people are transformed into scared,
wounded, insecure individuals.

In a very understanding and concise way, Rev Ronald T Smith
in his book *Annulment: A Step-by-step Guide for Divorced Catholics* guides those Catholics who have been divorced and who
wish to marry again with the blessings of the Catholic Church. It
is also written for those divorced Catholics who may not wish to
remarry at this time, but who want to bring a greater degree of
closure to their previous marriage.

He writes:

*This book will help you understand the annulment process and
enable you to find healing, peace and the strength to move forward with your life in a positive manner. Besides offering step-by-
step instructions to help you complete the sometimes confusing
annulment procedure, it also offers suggestions about restoring
your relationship with your family, your friends and your God.*

*A decree of annulment does not say that a marriage ended in
divorce. Rather, it says that, in the eyes of the Catholic Church, a
sacramental marriage never existed, it is the belief of the Catholic
Church that this couple was never married. Because the two people were not married, they are free to marry someone else in the
Catholic Church.*

*Much confusion arises over the meaning of an annulment and
its relationship to a civil divorce and to the legitimacy of the chil-*

dren that may have been born during the time the couple was considered married. There are several important points to keep in mind:

1. An annulment is a decree of the Church. It has no civil effect. Thus a person cannot begin the Church's annulment process until after he or she has been granted a civil divorce.

2. An annulment (also called a "decree of nullity") is a decree of the Catholic Church that a valid sacramental marriage did not exist between the two people. They may have lived as husband and wife for many years. They may even have had children, but in the eyes of the Church, they did not have a valid sacramental marriage.

3. When the Church grants an annulment it does not render the children illegitimate.

Divorced people are often plagued by the "what ifs". What if I had been more forgiving, prayed more, sought counselling sooner, and on and on?

As you look back at your marriage and its breakup and examine the guilt you feel, try to objectively determine the actual degree of guilt. If the feeling of guilt is groundless, then it is time to let go of it, realizing that God understands it was beyond your control and ability to this commitment. If your feelings of guilt are based on actual fact and the result was something you did to break up the marriage, then forgive yourself.

In any event, it is my hope that any person who finds themselves in this position will receive help in his or her individual situation, as divorced Catholics should never feel that the doors of the Church are closed to them.

My heartfelt appeal is that persons who find themselves in this position to have the courage to take the next step...... to approach the Church for an annulment of your marriage.

Addictions

Need I list the addictions of today's world? Alcohol, drugs, pornography, smoking, gambling, obesity, prescription medicines, shopping, work, exercise, money, status, social media, i-Pads, smartphones and X-boxes and even religion – these come readily to mind but no doubt there are many others.

An addiction is a compulsive self-destructive behaviour that enslaves or holds a person from experiencing life. When someone is addicted it brings shame, feelings of not being worthy and loved to the person, family, friends and beyond to the community and the workplace.

What does my generation know about the addictions in the modern world other than they are very sadly very common in society today? It was also a problem for our generation but somehow it seems much more serious with the present generation, with rampant youth unemployment, lack of a father figure in the home and a general dropping of moral standards in homes, schools, businesses and politics.

So I Googled to get a current take on addictions but I must warn against this practice even though is useful to get fairly good information. It must not take the place of good old common sense and consulting properly trained experts. When I had to undergo surgery for a hernia some years ago the surgeon warned me about consulting Dr Google because often you only get half the story. Nevertheless, it is a useful point of reference to start with.

These are some useful pointers according to an article in *Psychology Today* about addiction as it throws light on the subject:

Addiction is a condition in which a person engages in the use of a substance or in a behaviour for which the rewarding effects provide a compelling incentive to repeatedly pursue the behaviour despite detrimental consequences. Addiction may involve the use of substances such as alcohol, inhalants, opioids, cocaine, nicotine, and others or behaviours such as gambling; there is scientific evidence that the addictive substances and behaviours share a key neurobiological feature - they intensely activate brain pathways of reward and reinforcement, many of which involve the neurotransmitter dopamine.

Both substance use disorders and gambling behaviours have an increased likelihood of being accompanied by mental health conditions such as depression and anxiety or other pre-existing problems. Substance use and gambling disorders not only engage many of the same brain mechanisms of compulsivity they respond too many of the same approaches to treatment.

Complex conditions that affect reward, reinforcement, motivation, and memory systems of the brain, substance use and gambling disorders are characterised by impaired control over usage; social impairment, involving disruption of everyday activities and relationships and may involve craving. Continuing use is typically harmful to relationships and work and school obligations. Another distinguishing feature is that individuals may continue the activity despite physical or psychological harm incurred or exacerbated by use. And typically, tolerance to the substance increases, as the body adapts to its presence.

Because addiction affects the brain's executive functions, individuals who develop an addiction may not be aware that their behaviour is causing problems for themselves and others. Over time, the pursuit of the pleasurable effects of the substance or behaviour dominates an individual's activities.

There is no one cause of addiction. Although genetic or other biological factors may contribute to vulnerability to the condition, many social, psychological and environmental factors have a powerful influence on substance use. There is no one personality type associated with addiction, either. The lack of ability to tolerate distress or other strong feelings is linked to addiction.

Although all addictions have the capacity to induce a sense of hopelessness and feelings of failure, as well as shame and guilt, research documents that recovery is a rule rather than the exception, and that there are many routes to recovery. Individuals can achieve physical, psychological, and social functioning on their own – so-called natural recover; others prefer the support of community or peer-based networks. Still others opt for clinical-based recovery through the services of credentialed professionals.

The road to recovery is seldom straight: Relapse, or recurrence of substance use, is common- but definitely not the end of the road. For those who achieve remission of the disorder for five years, scientists report, the likelihood of relapse is no greater than that among the general population.

Alcoholics Anonymous is an international mutual aid fellowship founded in 1935 by Bill Wilson and Bob Smith in Akron, Ohio. Its stated purpose is to enable its members to stay sober and help other alcoholics achieve sobriety.

Their standard prayer is recited at each of their meetings to publicly accept spiritual awakening and "acceptance" of a "higher power" to help in the abstraction and abstinence from alcohol.

Grant me the serenity to accept the things I cannot change
Courage to change the things I can, and
Wisdom to know the difference.

It can be very hard to get over your addiction, especially when you are struggling to overcome it on your own. But, no matter how impossible it seems at the beginning, you can recover from your addiction if you have the right support structure and treatment and prayer.

However, before you can overcome it, you must first admit and accept that you **have** an addiction. Recovery is not easy but you can do it! Overcoming your addiction works better if it's combined with treatment and support from loved ones.

Beating an addiction doesn't happen overnight. You need to be ready to let go of your addiction by firstly changing your lifestyle completely. This means changing your daily routine, who you hang out with and what you put in your body. This makes your recovery easier and makes it easier to overcome your addiction.

The choice to quit needs to come from you and no one else - **you** need to make that change.

There will be many triggers and temptations that will make you want to continue with the addiction - your old friends who want to chill with you again, your lack of outside interests like sport, hobbies, reading, lack of serious motivation at work, lack of application to your studies and advancing your career, not developing new interests and genuine friendships and not being involved in the community and Church. You need to build enough strength to say "no".

Once you have made that decision to stop with your addiction and you are determined to live a better life again, with help, you can walk away from your addiction.

You will have to learn to cope with stress and negative events in your life – without having to resort to addictions to numb your pain. In order to keep yourself from going back to your addictions, use stress-reduction techniques like eating and drinking right, exercising, reading, volunteering. Whether it's joining a church-based group or other social support network, playing sport, or joining a support group and connecting with other people who have gone through similar experiences can add great value and help to your recovery efforts. It can also be a form of therapy for you.

Make sure you give yourself enough time to recover from your addiction and make sure it's at your own pace, you are not competing against anyone.

Overcoming your addiction is not easy but it is possible. If you want to give up make contact with someone immediately – your support group, your family, and your spiritual advisor.

What you do in your free time and most importantly how you think about yourself helps you in your commitment to changing many things in your life.

The decision to overcome your addiction has to come from you first. So if you have decided that you have had enough and you want to live a better life, seek help. The sooner you seek help, the sooner you can recover.

Some research reported by The National Center on Addiction and Substance Abuse suggests that some "behavioural addictions" involve similar changes in the brain, common risk factors and behaviours. They also show common responses to certain types of treatment. These findings suggest the possibility that addiction may be one disease with different forms of expression. Among people with a substance problem there is evidence that they have multiple substance disorders which shows startling effects:

Nicotine: Over 1 in 5 have another alcohol or drug problem

Alcohol: Nearly 1 in 3 also have a nicotine or other drug problem

Illegal drugs: Nearly 2 in 3 have another substance problem

Prescription drugs: Nearly 3 in 4 have another substance problem.

There are signs to watch out for in order to try and prevent abuse or take timely intervention if the abuse has taken hold in a person. Firstly, if there is direct evidence of drug use through personal observation of the act of taking drugs, reports from others or through direct confession or admitting to drug use. Secondly, observing behaviour problems against a checklist of 11 – skipping school, college or varsity, absence from work, dropping out of sport or other activities, refusing to seek work, most friends are poor choices or bad influences, frequently coming home late at night, involvement in fights outside the family, trouble with the police, frequently starting arguments and/or fights with family members, frequently disrespectful to parents and/or grandparents, and frequently using vulgar and/or obscene language at home.

The 12 Steps of Alcoholics Anonymous (which can be applied equally to other addictions) are:

- *We admit we are powerless over alcohol – our lives have become unmanageable.*
- *We come to believe that a Power greater than ourselves can restore us to sanity.*
- *We make a decision to turn our will and our lives over to the care of God as we understand Him.*
- *We have made a searching and fearless moral inventory of ourselves.*
- *We admit to God, to ourselves and to other human beings the exact nature of our wrongs.*
- *We are entirely ready to have God remove all these defects of character.*
- *We humbly ask Him to remove our shortcomings.*
- *We have made a list of all persons we have harmed and are willing to make amends to them all.*
- *We have made direct amends to such people wherever possible, except when to do so would injure them or others.*
- *We will continue to take a personal inventory of ourselves and when we do wrong, promptly admit it.*
- *We will seek through prayer and meditation to improve our conscious contact with God as we understand Him, praying only for knowledge of His will for us and the power to carry that out.*
- *We have had a spiritual awakening as the result of these steps, we will try to carry this message to other alcoholics and we will practice these principles in all our affairs.*

Modern adaptations of the 12 steps to recovery are non-denominational and respect all religious beliefs, with the sole intent of solving the problem of a person's compulsive drinking problem. Anonymity and non-judgmental open-mindedness and sobriety are the prerequisites to every meeting of the alcoholic group.

We can turn to the Bible verse in Eccl 4:9-10 for inspiration to realise the important role members of the family must play in confronting and assisting with these challenges: *Better two than one alone, since thus their work is really rewarding. If one should fall, the other helps him up; but what of the person with no-one to help him when he falls?*

Theology of the Body

It is an illusion to think we can build a true culture of human life if we do not accept and experience sexuality and love and the whole of life according to their true meaning and their close-in interconnection. These words were penned by Pope John Paul II in *The Gospel of Life*.

Who am I? How do I find true happiness and fulfilment? These are fundamental questions in each of our lives. It quickly becomes clear, however, that the best the world can offer are counterfeits that wound, betray us, and leave us wanting. Our longings for love, intimacy, and freedom are good, but the sexual revolution sold us a bill of goods that simply cannot satisfy.

But there is real hope, and it comes in the form of John Paul ll's *Theology of the Body*.

In his book *Freedom – Twelve Lives Transformed by the Theology of the Body*, with an introduction by Christopher West, Matthew Pinto interviews a number of people who have discovered the meaning of their very existence. They have all realised that the message of the Theology of the Body is the key to understanding their purpose in this life.

They have found what we're all looking for – the authentic path to happiness and freedom.

Through twelve real-life stories, you will:
- See how the Theology of the Body gives you a "new lens" through which to see the world with great clarity.
- Learn how this teaching is uniquely capable of healing past spiritual and psychological wounds

- Discover how the journey to sexual integration, although challenging, will actually liberate all aspects of our lives
- Learn the extraordinary connections between human sexuality and the entire Catholic sacramental Order.
- See why persisting in sin ultimately leads to misery.
- Understand why "love" is the greatest of the three theological virtues.
- Marvel at God's powerful and healing grace in the lives of ordinary people.
- See that God's grace can prevail over any challenge in life.

Christopher West is recognised around the world for his work promoting an integral, biblical vision of human life, love, and sexuality and is the best-selling author of five books. He is one of the most sought-after speakers in the Church today. He says he discovered in reading the *Theology of the Body* that we are persons made to come into a loving and perfect communion with God and others. For most of his adult life, he had left God out. He had been duped into thinking human love was all he needed for happiness. Love for and from others is meant to help us experience a taste of God's love, but it is not a replacement. There is only one Love that completely satisfies. But once we realise that, how do we find it? How do we live it?

Yes, Pope St John Paul II said if we live according to the truth of our sexuality, we fulfil the very meaning of life. What is it? Jesus reveals it when he says: This is my commandant, that you love one another as I have loved you *(Jn 15:12)*.

How did Jesus love us? *This is my body which is given for you (Luke 22:19)*.

God created sexual desire as the power to love as he loves. And this is how the first couple experienced it. This is what is written in Gen 2:25: *they* were both naked, and were not ashamed.

As a sacrament, marriage is meant to symbolise the union of Christ and the Church (*Eph 5:31 -32*). The Body has a language that is meant to express God's free, total, faithful, and fruitful love. This is exactly what spouses commit to at the altar: Have you come here freely? To give yourselves to each other without reservation? Do you promise to be faithful until death? Do you promise to receive children lovingly from God? The priest asks these questions, to which the groom and the bride say yes.

In turn, spouses are meant to express this same *yes* with their bodies whenever they become one flesh. Indeed the very words: *"'I take you to be my wife (my husband)' can be fulfilled only by means of conjugal intercourse,"* says the Pope. Sexual union is meant to be the renewal of wedding vows!

Why is the Body a Theology*?*

We can't see God. As a pure Spirit, He is invisible. Yet Christianity is the religion of God's self-disclosure: In Christ, God has revealed his innermost secret: God himself is an eternal exchange of love, Father, Son, and Holy Spirit, and he has destined us to share in that exchange (CCC, 221).

Somehow the human body makes this eternal mystery of love visible. How? Specifically through the beauty of sexual difference and our call to union. God designed the union of the sexes as a created version of his own eternal exchange of love. And right from the beginning, the union of man and woman foreshadows our eternal destiny of union with Christ. As St Paul says in Eph 5:31-32: *one flesh*, and, union *is a great mystery, and I mean with reference to Christ and the Church.*

Death

Christians find bright rays of hope in the midst of their sadness at the loss of a member of the family or a friend. Everyone is sad, confused, stunned, and even overwhelmed by the loss.

There are bad moments when tears came regardless of efforts to try to control them. when words get stuck in your throat. But the wonderful support and words and embraces of family and friends, their prayers, their words of sympathy, their silent presence when they come personally to offer their condolences at home and their attendance at the funeral service all help to share your sorrow and grief. The tangible support is comforting, it will raise you from the depths and help you to carry on.

We, Christians, believe death is not the end, but a new beginning. Our loved ones have to pass through death to a glorious new life with God. A person who sought God on earth through faith will now see God face to face as He really is. Soon we will all be united, as we are told in 2 Cor 5:1 26, with those we love:

"In a dwelling provided for us by God in the heavens, not made by hands but to last forever in the heavens."

For all of us, there comes a last time for doing familiar things that we take for granted as we live our daily lives. There is the last time we see our family and friends. The last time we write a letter, a birthday card or send an email or WhatsApp, hear a word or name spoken. The last time we share a family meal together.

Perhaps it is a mercy that most of us don't know when the last time arrives, that we are never sure when our goodbye is the final farewell.

Even the dying can still hope that they will get well again; that they will feel the human touch again; that they will hear the curtains being drawn at night; that they will smell and enjoy a lovely breakfast in the morning.

The close friendship that Jesus had with his followers also came to an end. At their last meal, they celebrated together Jesus gave his disciples an everlasting gift. The gift was a surprise. Jesus gave himself– literally. We read in Mt 26:26 Jesus said: *"Take it, this is my body. This is my blood. I shall not drink any more wine until the day I drink the new wine in the Kingdom of God."*

When our daughter-in-law Debbie died suddenly after less than a day in hospital on 2nd December 2015 in Lincoln Park, New Jersey, her husband Trevor was at her bedside holding her hand. She had fought a courageous battle against cancer and lost. But she never lost her faith in God.

There is no knowing what her thoughts were in those last hours. She would have drawn comfort from the words from Rev 21:3-4: *"I heard a loud voice from the throne saying, 'Behold, God's dwelling is with the human race. He will dwell with them and they will be his people and God himself will always be their God. He will wipe away every tear from their eyes, and there shall be no more death or mourning, wailing or pain, for the old order has passed away."*

In these moments of deep sorrow, the support, prayers, house visits, messages of condolences from family, friends, fellow Christians, prayer groups and even complete strangers were simply overwhelming for Trevor and their three children Leah-Marie, Nicholas and Julia. Debbie was only 42 years old when she died.

We must continue to pray for our deceased family and relatives. Christians who have died continue to be members of the communion of saints. We believe that we can assist them by our prayers, and they can assist us by their prayers. Praying for the dead might not make sense to non-believers but for Christians, it is part and parcel of our faith tradition, rooted in Old and New Testament readings.

Growing Through the Years

In 1995 Toni Rowland founded the Catholic family magazine "*Marfam*" in South Africa. She retires in 2019 at the age of 74 and, in what could be the last issue, she reflects in her editorial how life has changed in the past 24 years.

After much personal reflection and discernment, she observes that there is more to family life than marriage, and even though we support the church's vision that marriage is the ideal basis for family life the reality has changed in families and the worshipping community.

This is the present position in our world, despite a vision of strong family focus from leaders and government. St John Paul II was adamant that the future of the Church and of the world was through the family. In the secular field, the South African Government too, holds this view, which is promoted through the Department of Social Development (DSD) Family Services Forum and the *White Paper on Families* - the national policy.

Toni Rowland makes some profound observations as she reflects on life, her own and life in general. She quotes Pope Francis AL295: "*The human being knows, loves and accomplishes moral good by different stages of growth.*"

She writes further:

That powerful African concept of ubuntu, *as compassion and acceptance of our humanity, makes one think. Is this something inherent in people or something that grows like the mustard seed? Situations and conditions in one's own family and others close by are a very definite part of the journey of life.*

Looking back over the years I have experienced many of "the joys and hopes, griefs and anxieties" mentioned in the Vatican II document Gaudium et Spes. *Some have been in my own birth family, our marriage and that of our children as well as in the extended family at a greater distance.*

Every family experiences births and death, illness and accidents but also the joy of love and achievement. That is normal. I think my inclination is to focus more on the crosses than the joys, the pain and hurt I see around me. Just in this one extended family of mine, there have been long and happy marriages, difficult marriages, co-habitation, divorce and early widowhood, early parental deaths, step-parents and step-children, depression, suicide, serious debilitating accidents, alcoholism and drugs, both success and failure in work and school, learning difficulties, wealth and poverty, as well as sexual orientation challenges.

We have all learned many lessons in life as couples, parents and grandparents, some that brought us closer to one another, some not. How well have we shared our stories? I think we could have done more.

Ultimately, we have matured and aged, can and do we look back with love and along with Pope Francis says, All of us should be able to say 'thanks to the experience of our life in the family we come to believe in the love God has for us'.

A family, small or extended, is a web of relationships, more or less close or intimate, yet still belonging in a unique but complex way.

Entering into a relationship is not just a couple thing, but also entry into this wider network, bringing one's own set of values and traditions. Mother-in-law, daughter-in-law *are ones that can take quite an adjustment. Marriage happens or maybe not in today's world, unlike in my early years. Maybe new couples will cohabit, even at any age, rather than take that more committed step.*

Marriage grows through stages. It is said that one makes 3.5 or more marriages to the same spouse as each person matures and adjusts to their situation in different ways. All marriages have their problems from time to time but will they pull through and survive these difficult times and how? Parents will stand by and suffer too while assisting where they can. How will children fit into a family's life pattern with their own particular needs and person-alities? Children come along, often by choice these days and we're happy and grateful if all is well. They grow and develop and aim to achieve what we and they hope and dream of. Here too grandparents play a role, large or small, close or distant, as this beloved little family might move away on their own.

Death, especially of a spouse, is the most traumatic event for the whole family because children lose a parent, grandchildren a grandparent and siblings too sense a loss. Will God be part of this experience?

A sadness for many, grandparents especially, is a drop in church participation of younger members. Is this a loss of faith or do we comfort ourselves with the knowledge that where there is love there is God?

Surely it is true that growing through the years is essential to become fully human, fully alive, yet never complete.

Boake Family Genealogy

We are aware that from known records we humans go back more than 5 000 years. Whilst it is important to understand our origins as Christians, there is a growing interest to trace our ancestry to more recent times as this gives us a better understanding of our family tree. Maybe we are worried about Charles Darwin's *Theory of Evolution* that espoused that humans descended from apes! So we, the current human species, just want to be sure that our ancestors were humans that we can identify with.

About 40 years ago I received a strange telephone call while at work in Johannesburg from a Dorothy Boake-Panzer in America. She had written a book, *The Beech Tree – the History of the Boake Family*, and was still continuing her research in particular into what had had happened to Dr Samuel Boake, our grandfather, who had emigrated to South Africa after fighting in World War I in the Australian army in the major battles in Europe.

I was never really told how Samuel Boake came to settle in the platteland of the Northern Transvaal, where he brought a farm called *"Papkuil"* outside Pietersburg and where he ran a medical practice in the town. His early history is recorded on page 77 of her book.

Dorothy was very excited to find my name *Boake, D I* in the telephone directory (Yellow Pages) as the only Boake name listed in South Africa so she wanted to know about my background. I first had to consult with my mother, Helen Margaret Hayward Boake, who was a mine of information, being the much-respected matriarch of the family. You could sense Dorothy's excitement as she gathered this long lost information - she had finished her story on the Boakes in South Africa on a rather sad note: *Dr Samuel Boake died some time after 1945, having lived to quite an old age. Nothing more was known about his family in Pietersburg, Transvaal, South Africa.*

I quote from the Foreword of Dorothy's book should a family member alive or some yet unborn great-grandchild wants a glimpse into the past or make a study of the Boake family history.

Talent, in the shape of people with superior gifts, always flies from an impoverished country to a new and potentially richer country. And that is why the centre of civilisation moved slowly from its Sumerian origin; as it has indeed been moving almost ever since.

We, as human beings, are the sum total of all those gone before us. This is applicable not only in the field of genetics but in education, religion, nationality, and even in politics. To deny our heritage is to deny ourselves. To know and understand our past, to study and appreciate our progenitors, to value and love those misty ancestors whose names we may never know but whose contributions are essential to the very skein of life, and to pass on to future generations our knowledge of this personal history is a challenge and an opportunity. Attempting to unravel the often twisted threads which make up the "webwork structure" of our past is an invigorating and rewarding experience.

We are especially fortunate because our forefathers had the daring and initiative to venture forth into new lands; first to Ireland from England, and then to land in the New World in both America and Canada. These ancestors were endowed with special attributes and talents which, combined with hard work and opportunities to pioneer, enabled them to create a life for themselves and their families unlike any other in the world had ever known. Their reasons for leaving the Old World, their reasons for settling in specific localities, their reasons for migrating westward during the great era of expansion; their choice of a religion, of an occupation, of an education for their children are all the threads that are woven into the complex pattern of human life.

This pattern, with its many-coloured, intricate interlacing and overlays, is carried on through generation after generation and is clearly apparent in us today; just the colour of our eyes, hair, skin, the shape of our bodies and the length of our noses is manifested in us through the pattern of our inherited gene structure.

Dorothy ends the Foreword of her book with a lovely dedication and an appeal to the Boakes the world over:

I, therefore, dedicate this book to all future generations into whose hands will fall the cherished memories of the past; and I charge you, beloved great-grandchildren, guard well your heritage!

There is no clear explanation where the name Boake came from. Some "so-called experts" put forward different theories. We find that Mark Anthony Lowes in his *"Dictionary of Family Names of the United Kingdom"* published in 1860, states that the name "Noakes" comes from "atten"(Old English for "at the") and "oakes" meaning a man who lives at the oak trees. He then continues to state that "Boake" is probably "By Oak" (By the oak tree). There seems no evidence to support this theory, just as there is no evidence to support the theory purported when he states that "Boake" comes from the northern form of "balk, a ridge (as a boundary)". George Black in *"Surnames of Scotland"* reports that Laing first finds the name "Boak" in the parish of Kirkcolm, Southwest Scotland, but he sees no evidence either that Boak could possibly have come from balk. Henry Harrison in *"Surnames of the United Kingdom"* lists "Boake....... (Eng)". "Boake....... (Dweller at the beech tree) ....Old English for beech tree is "boc".

It should be pointed out that Mr Harrison fails to note that Scandinavian for beech tree is "bok" and that the only areas in which the name Boak/Boake (Bok) was found were the places heavily settled by the Norwegian Vikings.

From time to time, I used to tell bedtimes stories to my grandchildren about the romantic past of our ancestors - that beginning in about 800 AD from the narrow rugged fjords, from the mists which covered the North Sea, from the less than fertile lands of Scandinavia, strong, daring and otherwise ruthless men ventured forth to raid the islands near their homeland. These Vikings were our ancestors and I am sticking to my story! This is real Irish storytelling coursing through my blood!

No doubt there is a new generation of Boakes not featured in *The Beech Tree* living in many parts of the world who have risen to prominence, and on whom we can rely to continue our proud heritage.

Two persons of completely contrasting attributes readily come to mind and are worth mentioning here if one is interested in trying to trace their ancestry. This is becoming popular nowadays as people are searching the internet as they are curious about the roots of their family and to understand themselves better.

Barcroft Henry Thomas Boake was born on 26th March 1866. He was a tough 19th-century Australian stockman and drover, while at the same time he was a sensitive if unstable, character. He wrote poetry about the injustices meted out to his fellow workers by usually uncaring, and often absent, land and stock owners. He seemed to be at home out in the bush and it was said that he looked better on a horse than off, so adept a horseman was he. He found quiet times during rest periods to write and it would be easy to speculate how great a poet he might have become had he lived longer. Tragically he hanged himself from a tree using his own stockwhip. He died in May 1892 aged just 26. His work was collected and published posthumously and critics have speculated on whether or not the best work was still to come from this tragic and troubled figure.

South African-born Robert Boake looks after the settings for arguably the biggest show in television - the award-winning *Game of Thrones* which premiered its seventh and penultimate season in July 2018. Being a keen photographer and a creative background in the arts was to provide him with a platform to grow. He identified the northern coastline and the Mourne Mountains as two elements of Northern Irish nature that play a pivotal role in the screen telling of George R R Martin's beloved novels.

So I took up Dorothy's challenge at the end of her book by asking my two older brothers, Jock and Colin, to gather as much information about the Boakes in South Africa as possible, to preserve this history for future generations in our neck of the woods. That reminds me - I need to prod the twins again before it is too late as Father Time is catching up with our generation.

The Nuts and Bolts of Modern Family Life

The importance of families staying together and supporting each other is critical for the survival and happiness of the human race.

Of all the leaders of the world, Pope Francis stands out as one of the very few who recognises that the major problem in the world today is the destruction of family life. He looks at the nuts and bolts of family life in his Apostolic Exhortation titled *Amoris Laetitia* (The Joy of Love).

The background to the Exhortation is explained in plain and simple language, which gives an insight into the reasons for its issue in the Jubilee Year of Mercy in these passages as quoted:

5. First, because it represents an invitation to Christian families to value the gifts of marriage and families, and to persevere in a love strengthened by the virtues of generosity, commitment, fidelity and patience. Second, because it seeks to encourage everyone to be a sign of mercy and closeness wherever family life remains imperfect or lacks peace and joy.

6. I will begin with an opening chapter inspired by the Scripture, to set a proper tone. I will then examine the actual situation of families, in order to keep firmly grounded in reality, I will go on to recall some essential aspects of the Church's teaching on marriage and the family, thus paving the way for two central chapters dedicated to love. I will then highlight some pastoral approaches that can guide us in building sound and fruitful homes in accordance with God's plan, with a full chapter devoted to the raising of children. Finally, I will offer an invitation to mercy and the pastoral discernment of those situations that fall short of what the Lord demands of us, and conclude with a brief discussion of family spirituality.

7. It is my hope that, in reading this text, all will feel called to love and cherish family life, for families are not a problem; they are first and foremost an opportunity."

The Pope does not mince words when he says we need to be alert to "*the growing danger represented by an extreme individu-*

alism which weakens family bonds and ends up considering each member of the family as an isolated unit, leading to the idea that one's personality is shaped by his or her desires which are considered absolute".

Put simply, it's the old problem of *'me, myself and I'*. Yes, it may be true that the modern human sciences have helped us to recover the dignity and importance of the individual as someone to be valued in his and her own right but at the same time, we can't deny the tensions created by a culture of individualism and materialism. These lead to intolerance and hostility in families.

As Pope Francis puts it so realistically: "*One of the most obvious manifestations of this individualism is found in the 'cyber-effect' the way computer and internet technology impacts upon human culture and behaviour. We all witness daily the down-side of a 'virtual' experience of life.*"

Here I think of the speed with which people move from one effective relationship to another. They believe, along the lines of social networks, that love can be connected or disconnected at the whim of the consumer, and a relationship quickly 'blocked'. I think too, of the fears associated with permanent commitment, the obsession with free time.

Rooted as he is in the Gospel values of Jesus and the very best of Catholic social teaching, the Pope laments the way we treat human relationships like we treat material objects: *Everything is disposable; everyone uses and throws away, takes and breaks, exploits and squeezes to the last drop. Then, goodbye.*

No matter how dramatically we have definite opposing viewpoints in personal, business and political matters, it is important to remember that those who differ from you and are possibly wrong, are still human beings deserving your respect. Always remain civil, deal with the issues and avoid being personal.

Our faith as Christians provides the perfect antidote. We reject selfishness and arrogance. We believe in self-sacrifice and commitment. We imitate Jesus in his humble service of others and like him, we are willing to give ourselves generously to others.

Where more in family life do we learn that individuals cannot act privately and arbitrarily without reference to the needs, dignity and rights of others?

In Chapter 2 titled *"The Experiences and Challenges Facing Family Life,"* the Pope touches on a few relevant points of the new challenges facing families:

50. The first is the raising of children. He understands that parents come home from work exhausted, not wanting to talk. Families no longer share a common meal. Distractions abound, including addiction to television. This makes it all the more difficult for parents to hand on their faith to their children. Other responses pointed to the effect of severe stress on families, who often seem more caught up with securing their future than enjoying the present. This is a broader cultural problem, aggravated by fears about steady employment, finances and the future of children.

51. Drug use was also mentioned as one of the scourges of our time, causing immense suffering and even breakup for many families. The same is true of alcoholism, gambling and other addictions. The family could be the place where these are prevented and overcome, but society and politics fail to see families at risk. We see the serious effects of this breakdown in families torn apart, the young uprooted and the elderly abandoned, children who are orphans of living parents, adolescents and young adults confused and unsupported. As the Bishops of Mexico have pointed out, violence within families breeds new forms of social aggression, since family relationships can also explain the tendency to a violent personality. This is often the case with families where communication is lacking, defensive attitudes predominate, the members are not supportive of one another, family activities that encourage participation are absent, the parental relationship is frequently conflictual and violent, and relationships between parents and children are marked by hostility. Violence within the family is a breeding-ground of resentment and hatred in the most basic human relationships.

52. No one can think that the weakening of the family as that natural society founded on marriage will prove beneficial to society as a whole. The contrary is true: it poses a threat to the mature growth of individuals, the cultivation of community values and the moral progress of cities and countries. There is a failure to realise that only the exclusive and indissoluble union between a man and woman has a plenary role to play in society as a stable commitment that bears fruit in new life. We need to acknowledge the great variety of family situations that can offer a certain stability. But de facto or same-sex unions, for example, may not simply be equated with marriage. No union that is temporary or closed to the transmission of life can ensure the future of society. But nowadays, who is making an effort to strengthen marriages, to help marries couples overcome their problems, to assist them to work of raising children and, in general, to encourage the stability of the marriage bond?

53. Some societies still maintain the practice of polygamy; in other places, arranged marriages are an enduring practice. In many places, not only in the West , the practice of living together before marriage is widespread , as well as a type of cohabitation which totally excludes any intention to marry. In various countries, legislation facilitates a growing variety of alternatives to marriage, with the result that marriage, with its characteristics of exclusivity, indissolubility and openness to life, comes to appear as an old fashioned and outdated option. Many countries are witnessing a legal deconstruction of the family, tending to adopt models based almost exclusively on the autonomy of the individual will.

Surely it is legitimate and right to reject older forms of the traditional family marked by authoritarianism and even violence, yet this should not lead to a disparagement of marriage itself, but rather to the rediscovery of its authentic meaning and its renewal. The strength of the family lies in its capacity to love and teach how to love. For all the family's problems, it can always grow, beginning in love.

54. In this brief overview, I would like to stress the fact that, even though significant advances have been made in the recognition of women's rights and their participation in public life, in some countries, much remains to be done to promote these rights. Unacceptable customs still need to be eliminated. I think particularly of the shameful ill-treatment to which women are sometimes subjected, domestic violence and various forms of enslavement which, rather than a show of masculine power, are craven acts of cowardice. The verbal, physical, and sexual violence that women endure in some marriages contradicts the very nature of the conjugal union. I think of the reprehensible genital mutilation of women practiced in some cultures, but also of their lack of equal access to dignified work and roles in decision-making. History is burdened by the excesses of patriarchal cultures that consider women inferior, yet in our own day, we cannot overlook the use of surrogate mothers and the exploitation and commercialisation of the female body in the current media culture. There are those who believe that many of today's problems have arisen because of feminine emancipation. This argument, however, is not valid, it is false, untrue, a form of male chauvinism. The equal dignity of men and women makes us rejoice to see old forms of discrimination disappear, and within families there is a growing reciprocity. If certain forms of feminism have arisen which we must consider inadequate, we must nonetheless see in the women's movement the working of the Spirit for a clearer recognition of the dignity and rights of women.

55. Men play an equally decisive role in family life, particularly with regard to the protection and support of their wives and children. Many men are conscious of the importance of their role in the family and live their masculinity accordingly. The absence of a father gravely affects family life and the upbringing of children and their integration into society. This absence, which may be physical, emotional, psychological and spiritual, deprives children of a suitable father figure.

56. Yet another challenge is posed by the various forms of an ideology of gender that denies the difference and reciprocity in nature of a man and a woman and envisages a society without sexual differences, thereby eliminating the anthropological basis of the family. This ideology leads to educational programs and legislation enactments that promote a personal identity and emotional intimacy radically separated from the biological difference between male and female. Consequently, human identity becomes the choice of the individual, one which can also change over time. It is a source of concern that some ideologies of this sort, which seek to respond to what are at times under stable aspirations, manage to assert themselves as absolute and unquestionable, even dictating how children should be raised. It needs to be that biological sex and the socio-cultural role of sex (gender) can be distinguished but not separated. On the other hand, the technological revolution in the field of human procreation has introduced the ability to manipulate the reproductive act, mak-

ing it independent of the sexual relationship between a man and a woman. In this way, human life and parenthood have become modular and separable realities, subject mainly to the wishes of individuals or couples. It is one thing to be understanding of human weakness and the complexities of life, and another to accept ideologies that attempt to sunder what are inseparable aspects of reality. Let us not fall into the sin of trying to, replace the Creator. We are creatures, and not omnipotent. Creation is prior to us and must be received as a gift. At the same time, we are called to protect our humanity, and this means, in the first place, accepting it and respecting it as it was created.

57. I thank God that many families , which are far from considering themselves perfect, live in love, fulfil their calling and keep moving forward, even if they fall many times along the way. The Synod's reflections show us that there is no stereotype of the ideal family, but rather a challenging mosaic made up of many different realities, with all its joys, hopes and problems. The situations that concern us are challenges. We should not feel trapped into wasting our energy in doleful lament, but rather seek new forms of missionary creativity. In every situation that presents itself, the Church is conscious of the need to offers word of truth and hope. The great values of marriage and the Christian family correspond to a yearning that is part and parcel of human existence. If we see any number of problems, these should be, as the Bishops of Colombia have said, a summons to revive our hope and to make it a source of prophetic visions, transformative actions and creative forms of charity.

Looking at the present and future generations I am very concerned about what role God will play in family life unless the Church adapts to the changes as technological modernity detaches from social modernity in a disastrous way. I may be accused of being over pessimistic but the immediate future is a watershed moment for families.

On the Chemin de Compostelle, a pilgrimage from Le Puy to Saint-Jean-Pied-de-Port in France in September 2017 with our retired priest Fr John Finlayson and Lynne, I came across these words of wisdom, attributed to Antoine De Saint Exupery, on a wooden signpost which read: *"We do not inherit the Earth from our ancestors, we borrow it for our children".*

I don't think our present generation is really overly concerned about the world we hand over to future generations.

Social Media

This is something that has swept the world off its feet with no end in sight.

Think of the development of social media over the past 10 years and what is in the pipeline and apply that to all aspects of our daily lives, then add the unknowable, and the lives of humans will change in a drastic way.

Technology is unbelievably complicated, but how this will affect the basics of modern existence and deficient civilisation the future is simply not known or quantifiable. Then try and imagine how God slots into our daily living, the absence of whom is unthinkable if we are to live our lives in accordance with God's plan for us humans.

Fourth Industrial Revolution - AI

Try to assess what impact smart connected technology, which will transform our lives dramatically, will have on the families of the future.

I quote from the UK *The Tech* (Issue August 27th 2017), a supplement of *The Sunday Times Magazine*, for some indicators what the likely future will be:

We are into what many call 'the fourth industrial revolution' where artificial intelligence (AI) is walking off the pages of sci-fi books and into our lives. The first being steam engines, the second oil and electricity and the third computers. The only difference, analysts say, is this new revolution is likely to be 10 times faster, 300 times the scale and have 3 000 times the impact of the others, because once computers invade the physical world and start making autonomous, intelligent decisions, the opportunities are limitless.

But the pace of change is making many wonder whether this new force will, overall, be good for us, our families, our homes and our workplaces. For all the magic that self-driving cars and virtual butlers promise, could smart machines outsmart us and start pushing us around, before finally pulling the plug on us?

Yuval Harari, author of Homo Deus: A Brief History of Tomor-row, *thinks so. If we create robots that can do everything better than us, we could 'lose our economic and political value', he warns. David Autor, professor of economics at the Massachusetts Institute of Technology wonders if 'robocalypse is upon us' so should we welcome the bots or fear them?*

Despite all the economic growth and employment opportunities proponents say AI will generate, few doubt it will also spell redundancy for many. A new report by the National Bureau of Economic Research in the United States quantifies the problem in stark terms. Its authors, the economists Daron Acemoglu (MIT) and Pascual Restrepo (Boston University), argue jobs are already being lost to AI and are unlikely to come back. Between 1990 and 2007, the addition of each robot into US manufacturing resulted in the loss, on average, of 6.2 human jobs. You'll soon see this happening on your local building site. Robots called Sam (semi-automatic mason) are already beginning to replace brickies in America and will arrive here any day now. They can lay up to 3 000 bricks a day compared with the human average of 500 – all without fag breaks!

Automation will help us if we are one of the unlucky few who do still crash our cars or simply fall ill. Bots study x-rays, MRI scans, medical research papers and other data and pick up signs of disease that doctors sometimes miss. Back in Britain, thanks to another piece of AI– the autopilot of a Virgin Boeing 787 Dreamliner – I meet Lord Darzi, the surgeon who pioneered keyhole and robotic procedures. In his office at St Mary's Hospital in Paddington, he tells me robots can also perform better surgery than humans – and he's one of the best!

Robots are more precise, have a greater range of movement in keyhole surgery and no hand tremor, which makes stitching easier, he says.

John Hawksworth, chief economist at PwC, estimates that almost a third of existing UK jobs may be automated away in the next 15 years. That's a lot – and it's not merely 'routine jobs'. Professional services, once considered immune from the ravages of AI by smug white-collar workers, are also threatened. Automated services such as SimpleTax, KasFlow and Rocket Lawyer, which prepare our annual accounts and tax returns and do simple legal tasks, are putting human lawyers and accountants out of work. Even bosses are catching a whiff of their own professional mortality. "Chief executive officers feel reasonably confident we are not going to be replaced by artificial intelligence," Inga Beale, CEO of Lloyds of London insurance market, said recently. "But I'll sure there will be a time."

The job losses could herald a new era of unprecedented inequality. Humanity could split into a small class of 'superhumans' who control the AI that will run the lives of the huge underclass of 'useless people', says Yuval Harari. If that happens, social revolt won't be far behind, the president of the New America Foundation, Anne-Marie Slaughter recently argued. 'Remember, the first industrial revolution gave us Marxism', she said.

Silicon Valley usually turns a blind eye to the havoc its revolutionary products wreak on traditional industries and communities. Monetise first, moderate later, is their mantra (if anyone bothers to complain). But amid allegations that they facilitate secret communications by terrorists and with all the scandals surrounding hacking, trolling, hate speech, fake news, advertising scams and murders streamed live on Facebook, tech firms are on the defensive. The last thing they want is to be blamed for job losses and inequality far greater than anything wrought by globalisation. So they are already trying to persuade us that AI will be what they would call 'net positive'.

First, they echo PwC's work, arguing that AI will create way more new jobs than it will destroy. They cite the example of telecoms. Sure – each advance, from fixed lines through fax to mobile phones and email, displace some types of workers. The typing pool is a distant memory. But the increase in new jobs has more than made up for those lost. Today, millions of people work as app developers, virtual-world designers, self-drive car researchers, designers and makers, ride-sharing drivers, social media marketers - jobs that not only did not exist but would have been difficult even to imagine 10 years ago, before AI took off. 'We will have more and better jobs' predicts Marco Annunziata, chief economist at the giant US firm General Electric.

Most will involve working with robots to create what analysts call 'augmented intelligence' jobs. Collaboration, techno-optimists predict, will kick-start 'a renaissance, a golden age' in which

---

we will 'solve problems that were in the realm of science fiction', Amazon boss and billionaire, Jeff Bezos, likes to say and he knows a thing or two about predicting the future:

"In the short term, however, few dispute that many ordinary workers are likely to be left behind. Not every former taxi driver in Blackburn can become or wants to become a robot nurse supervisor in Woking. For those who lose out, Silicon Valley proposes something radical – 'a universal basic income.'"

The idea is that governments hugely increase the welfare using tax revenue, much of it derived from the highly profitable tech firms that politicians would have to force to cough up their fair share, not dodge it, as they now try to. Everyone would receive the minimum they need to live, regardless of whether they have a job. So, if you lost your job or simply did not want one, you could do something else: 'Imagine 6bn -10bn people doing nothing but arts and sciences, culture and exploring and learning. What a world that would be!'

The idea of universal basic income makes Steve Hilton of Crowdpac so angry he says: "Doing meaningful work and being rewarded for it is a basic human need. Depriving people of that is morally evil. It's revoltingly patronising for the great geniuses of Silicon Valley to say we can continue our fascinating work and earn vast incomes, so we can live in our gated communities guarded by robots and drones. But, sadly, you won't. Don't worry, though we'll pay you not to work."

He had a point. From an early age, we learn that jobs are central to family life and society as a whole. Waking up early and going to work is what our mum and dad do or did, what we do and what we tell our children they will do, too. We do it because it means we can take care of ourselves and our families and join the ranks of the "strivers" who politicians and newspapers tell us are morally superior to the "shirkers" living on Benefits Street. Jobs also enable us to learn new skills, make friends and, for many of us, to find our life partners. Homebrew and poetry only go so far.

Ghost shops. Ghost cars. Ghost everything? Welcome to the second machine age.

Chapter 6
New Challenges In Retirement

Facing Old Age

Growing old beats the alternative of dying young.

I recently came across an interesting article on old age in the Comboni bi-monthly magazine *Worldwide* which is an amazing magazine, thought-provoking, insightful with wide-ranging fascinating articles by different contributors, with outstanding pictures which grab your attention as you pore over the readings of your choice.

The article by Winnie Graham, a former journalist, interested me because we are of the same vintage, more or less, we both have four grown-up children with families scattered over the world. We both grew up on a farm and attended boarding school in Pietersburg (now Polokwane) in the old Northern Transvaal and were subjected to a strict boarding house routine which has influenced our way of life and thinking throughout our adult lives.

She writes:

Old age is no piece of cake. Retirement does not always give us more freedom because of loneliness and limitation of movement. Hardships and challenges are part of life – and of old age. Death is not the end; it's a new beginning that requires preparation. In the meantime, life goes on: we have to get out of bed in the mornings, prepare breakfast, wash the dishes, and clean the house. It will come to an end one day. Only God knows when.

In the many years since I was born in 1939 life has changed inordinately. How well I remember when my father wanted to phone to keep in touch with his mother on the family farm. She had a "party line" which everyone in the region shared. (No private calls in those days!) All the neighbours listened in and this was a constant source of friction in the community.

When I celebrated my 80th birthday a few months ago, I was inundated with new clothes from my children. I wanted to say: 'You shouldn't spend your money like this, I have enough to last me for the rest of my life.' Yet, I still could not bring myself to admit that my life was running to a close.

I could live another two years, maybe five or ten, but the greater part of my life is over. I have had my allotted span (three score years and ten). I've reared my children and worked for more years than I care to remember. Life has had its ups and downs but, truth be known, I have been blessed.

Old age is not a depressing thought. I've been through good times and bad but life has always been interesting and challenging. Now, I find myself looking up old friends recalling the happy times we once shared but talk more about how times have changed. But many have moved away to live with their children, and, sadly, many others have gone to meet our Maker.

Everyone has plans for retirement, but we are in God's waiting room, on standby for his call. The thought is not depressing. The moment will come – just as a train or bus will pull in – and we have to be ready for the ride.

Happiness and Joy

In the world of today in which we strive to lead meaningful lives, we face a flood of toxic emotions. We experience sadness, fear and anger, which saps our energy and leads to exhaustion physically, spiritually and mentally.

One of the successful ways of combating these emotions is to concentrate on thoughts and activities that lead to feelings of happiness and joy. To succeed we need to rid ourselves of toxic thinking. Our emotions all flow from the thoughts we allow ourselves to think. We are seeking peace of soul.

Happiness is the by-product of a meaningful life. The senses play a part in this. We should delight in a delicious meal with a bottle of good wine with family and friends. We all like to have suitable clothing for the seasons. The scent of waves pounding against the rocks or clambering up the mountains lifts our moods.

Joy, on the other hand, emerges from deep within the soul. Joy is the state of peace that comes from being in harmony with God's will. The sight of a majestic sunset makes us grateful to God for the gift of beauty.

St Augustine said: *Our hearts are restless until they rest in Thee, O Lord.* This rest may seem like a distant goal, but the truth is you can find it in the Lord anytime you choose. You can take a moment to ask him for the spiritual rest you need.

The first step is to stop your frantic thinking. Listen to your breathing. Reflect on God's love within you. The joy that will follow is the simplest form of gratitude.

Escaping from the toxic thinking that weighs you down, is the first step to attaining happiness and joy. It is a matter of being in touch with God's joy, Prayer will open your receptivity to the gift of Divine Joy.

Joy transcends the noise of the world. The state of spiritual gladness will soon purify your former mental swamp, and you will feel God's peace.

I can personally relate to this. I started off my working career in 1958, after leaving school, when I arrived at Johannesburg Station on a chilly morning with a battered suitcase containing my worldly possessions and full of determination and hope. Looking back over the past 79 years I freely acknowledge that I have been truly blessed with the Lord, always in my life, urging me on to persevere with hard work and diligent studies, as I have learnt from hard experience that there is no such thing as a free lunch in life. Despite the many hardships, challenges and setbacks I have no regrets.

We seem to have the wrong outlook on life because of the pressures and demands of the modern world which prevents us from enjoying living and experiencing life to the fullest – it doesn't really matter if we are happy or sad – enjoy the moment and move on.

I came across *Joy* by Fr Louis Evely very recently and it ties in with my own outlook on how we should live our lives with joy and a positive outlook. It was published in 1965 and sold for 75p, with the reviewer commenting: *A stimulating read with a sense of active concern about the real world, a spirituality that is biblical and robust, and avoidance of sentimentality, bloated language and traditional piety.*

Here are snippets from the book to reflect on:

In this age of "God death" God is indeed alive, but it is easy for us to miss because He is so much more alive than we are apt to be. While we go looking for Him with half hearts and tired wills, He, especially in the person of Christ, is already out and about, trying to share with us His life and joy.

I am going to talk about the joy of God – the joy He left us.

Jesus told us: 'Peace I leave with you; my peace I give you; not as the world gives do I give (Jn 14, 27).

But he told us also: 'These things I have spoken to you, that my joy may be in you, and that your joy may be full (Jn 15, 11)'.

Your sorrow will turn to joy (Jn 16, 20).

When you have become penetrated with the joy of God, all your sorrows will turn into joy, all of your trials will be graces; you will recognize your faults, you will be sorry for them, and they will be forgiven so they may become happy faults. They will remind you only of the goodness, the tenderness, the joy with which God forgives them.

When you become penetrated with the joy of God, God will become God again, he will become a Father again, and we will again become His children.

The Christian religion is a religion of joy. The Gospel is the Good News, and in spite of our occasionally melancholy appearance, we are messengers of joy, witnesses of the resurrection.

Christian joy differentiates us from the world and is the means of our apostolate: 'Truly, truly, I say to you, you will weep and lament, but the world will rejoice; you will be sorrowful, but your sorrow will turn into joy (Jn 16, 20)'.

Indeed, Christ made us the depositories of his joy.

What have we done with his joy?

Strangely enough, we do not cherish the joy of God. We are much more inclined to mourn with Christ than to rejoice with him.

How To Retire Happy

It is a fact that people are living longer because of enhanced medical care, more consciousness of healthy eating habits and a greater awareness of the need to exercise our bodies and especially our minds.

But do we plan for these extra years to ensure these are happy and stress-free and meaningful to ourselves, our families and our communities?

The question each person has to ask themselves is how to retire happy.

Here is a quotation from Gail Sheehan which hopefully is not the case, but can be applied to this important aspect of your life if planning for retirement is not properly addressed:

"When men reach their sixties and retire, they go to pieces. Women go right on cooking!"

There is a must-read book *How to Retire Happy and Free* by Ernie J Zelinski for all retirees; it sets out retirement wisdom that you won't get from your financial advisor. I started to read this at Barnes and Noble, the famous book shop in New Jersey, whilst drinking cups of coffee while Lynne went shopping, something I try to avoid, like most men. I took photos of some pages that appealed to me on my cell phone to read later then decided to include the advice given in my own book to pass on as it was of great practical value:

For the financial advisor, the financial considerations are always foremost in the planning for retirement. The first question posed is: Can I afford to retire? As a rule of thumb you must plan to receive 75% of your final earnings from employment in the form of dividends, interest, annuities and part-time work and, if that is insufficient, you may have to draw on your capital to bridge the shortfall. But the recommendation is that you must try and limit your drawings from your capital to 5% per year to cater for inflation and living longer in retirement. This also presupposes that your home is bond free, that you have a good medical aid, you are relatively healthy but more importantly that you consciously elim-

inate all unnecessary monthly expenses considered as unafford-able luxury in your retirement. The capital investment amount required at retirement age is calculated at roughly 10 times the annual income required to produce the required income. Sadly it is estimated that 95% of all persons going on retirement do not have the required capital to retire comfortably and maintain the standard of living enjoyed immediately prior to going on retire-ment.

You need to understand that's there far more to achieving fulfill-ment in retirement than having wealth and good health. Indeed, there is no shortage of scholarly evidence that financial status constitutes only a small piece of the puzzle as to whether people will succeed and will be happy in retirement. Apparently, most re-tirement planners either are not aware of this evidence or focus only on the financial aspect so that they can sell more financially related products.

Contrary to popular wisdom, many elements – not just having a million or two in the bank- contribute to happiness and satis-faction for today's retirees. Indeed, physical well-being, mental well-being and solid social support play bigger roles than finan-cial status for most retirees".

Retirement is the perfect time to become the person you would like to be and do the things you have always wanted to do. No doubt doing everything you have always wanted sounds great. It won't happen by itself, however. This is true even if you have ex-cellent health and a big pile of money in the bank when you retire.

Planning is important. You must take steps to ensure that when the bell rings to announce your retirement, you are ready for what's in front of you. The time for marital, personal, social, cre-ative and family activities expands considerably when the hours previously taken up with full-time employment cease.

How you manage time is just as important when you are in the workforce?

This I can assure you: You won't find genuine joy and satisfaction by spending all your time sleeping, relaxing, loafing, playing golf, travelling and watching TV, hoping to live to the ideal of a true idler. Many retired people with nothing to do wind up depressed and hating retirement. In this regard, Florida physician Richard

Neubauer concluded that many people experience a rapid decline in physical and mental health soon after retirement, often due to idleness and feelings of uselessness.

To retire happy, wild and free you must stay active. Retirement can be time for life's best moments, provided you take time to plan what you are going to do with the rest of your life. Just as important, you must be motivated enough to follow your dreams and change course if adversity intrudes to put a dent in your plans. The most fortunate of retirees are those who through good planning, experimentation and risk-taking succeed in making retirement the best time of their lives".

In short, it's up to you to design a lifestyle that is as relaxing and invigorating as you want it to be. No one else is going to do it for you. Recreating yourself as a retired person will be challenging for you, but through patience and positive thinking, you can do it. The rewards will be more than worth it.

As a matter of course, retirement is the last opportunity for individuals to invent themselves, let go of the past, and find peace and happiness within. Many people discover, much to their surprise, that retirement life following four or five decades of full-time work is full of new and exciting opportunities. For these individuals, their work was a barrier to the lives they wanted: now they are free to live life to the fullest.

Retirement is an opportune time to get to know yourself better - psychologically, materially and spiritually. Moreover, retirement allows you to do what you don't like as little as possible and what you like as much as possible. Whatever it is – a part-time career, family relationships, spiritual fulfillment, passionate pursuits, or the opportunity to hang around Starbucks writing a book you must find those things that matter most to you.

One of the activities open to retirees is helping others by volunteering to do charitable work. This creates feelings of achievement, responsibility, personal growth and recognition in your community. The result is satisfaction and happiness that no amount of money can buy. "The miracle is not that we do this work, but that we are happy to do it.

Age, as many retirees, soon-to-be retirees and wannabe retirees will be happy to hear, is not all it's made out to be. It is how you look at it. As a matter of course, retirement is often associated with old age, even though it shouldn't be. The fact is, however, if you are retired long enough, sooner or later some people will think of you as an older person. Whether you perceive yourself as having entered old age will depend upon your attitude more than anything else.

Plato tells us: *He who is of a calm and happy nature will hardly feel the pressure of age but to him who is of an opposite disposition youth and age are equally a burden.*

After all these years, experts are still trying to prove Plato right. In a study reported in the August 2002 issue of the *Journal of Personality and Social Psychology,* researchers claim that elderly people can actually think themselves into the grave a lot faster than they would prefer. Indeed, people with negative views about ageing shorten their lives by 7.6 years as compared with their counterparts who have a more positive view of life.

Surprisingly, a positive view about ageing can have a greater effect than good physical health. Psychologist Becca Levy of Yale University reported: *The effect of more positive self-perceptions of ageing on survival is greater than the physiological measures of low systolic blood cholesterol, each of which is associated with a longer lifespan to achieve.*

Taking Control of Your Life

So, as I come to the end of my working career and starting to feel physically and mentally exhausted – in fact at times I feel like a walking zombie just existing and mechanically going through the motions of going to work, taking one day at a time.

The cumulative aftermath of a number of recent events in my life was more draining on my well-being than I had realised. These included our long-lasting legal civil matter, when we were sued for about R40 million but which was finally decided in our favour by the Supreme Court of South Africa on the 30th November 2013 (reported in Motala v The Master (313/13)(2013) ZASCA 185 (29th November 2013); the criminal trial lasting 10 years, most of which time we were out on bail and strictly monitored by the Scorpions/National Prosecuting Authority (NPA) and which abruptly ended with the court pronouncement of a "not guilty" verdict on 13th December 2013; and, finally, my treatment for prostate cancer by hormone therapy, brachyther-apy needles and a course of radiation which was pronounced successful in April 2017.

There were times, in fact, that I felt as if I had been anaesthe-tised, as my brain seems to not to comprehend the actual seri-ousness of these life experiences.

But God has a way to help in these moments of severe stress and presents a plan to redirect one's direction in life.

Some years ago I was very excited to read a travel article in a magazine in the dentist's waiting rooms about the Camino pil-grimage to Santiago in Spain. I saw this as a huge challenge and a wonderful way to change focus onto something else and also to ease into retirement one day.

The story of the Camino is very interesting. The relics of Saint James the Greater, one of Christ's original apostles, were discov-ered at the beginning of the 9th century in Santiago de Compos-tela in Galicia in North West Spain. His remains were believed to have been miraculously transported there after his martyrdom in Jerusalem. The medieval cult of relics and spiritual powers gave rise to a number of great pilgrimage routes in the Middle Ages. Rome, Canterbury, Santiago de Compostela and even Jeru-salem were the most popular destinations.

For more than twelve centuries throngs of pilgrims have walked to Santiago. It was on this path, which had tributary routes in France converging through the Pyrenees, that many hostelries flourished. Pilgrim churches, many built in the Ro-manesque style, and holding the relics of other saints, were built and spectacularly expanded in towns and cities along the way.

St James the Greater was born in Bethsaida, the son of Zebe-dee and Salome and the brother of John the Apostle. Of all the Apostles, he was one of those that Jesus trusted most. After the death of Christ, James devoted himself to preaching in Judea and Samaria and, true to his mission of spreading the Good Word throughout all the lands, he decided to go and preach in the extreme west of the known world and embarked for Spain. It seems that he was not too successful in his preaching, although he may have trained a number of disciples to continue his work.

No truly historical evidence has come to light of St James' voyage to Spain. Many regard it as fallacious. It belongs more to legend than to history, as does the apparition in the flesh of the Virgin Mary while the Apostle was preaching in Spain.

Regarding legends and myths, a classical historian once said that *"these events never took place, although they exist forever".* The important significant thing about legends is not whether or not what they relate actually happened, but that people believe that they did. And so, for centuries people have believed that St James preached in Spain.

Back in Judea, after the relative failure of his mission, St James the Greater was beheaded by order of Herod Agrippa. A few of his disciples stole his body under cover of night and put it on a helm-less boat, placing his destiny in the hands of Divine Providence.

To add legend to legend, it was believed that the boat was made of stone, possibly the only one of its kind in history. It was thus made possible to verify when he reached his destination, a place on the coast of Galicia today called Padron, a name that derives from the piedra (stone) or Pedron to which it is said the boat was moored.

At the time when the Apostle's body reached the coast of Galicia, the territory was governed by a woman called Lupa. The disciples took St James' body from the boat and placed it on a great slab, which under the weight of the corpse caved in like wax to form a sepulchre. One of the disciples went to see Queen Lupa and asked her to help them to find a suitable burial ground. The place where the tomb was opened was called Libredon in memory of the queen's donation.

Eight centuries later, a hermit called Pelagio saw a star shine above the Libredon woods. He told the news to Teodomiro, Bishop of Iria Flavia, who, preceded by Pelagio and a host of shepherds and peasants, went to the woods and discovered, in the thicket of gorse, the ancient Roman-style chapel. The original chapel came to form the nucleus of the cathedral at Santiago.

I am always amazed by how I could have gone through life never having come across this incredible pilgrimage which goes right back to St James, one of the twelve Apostles, more than 2 000 years ago. Maybe the reason is that, growing up in South Africa, we are indeed isolated from the history of Christianity in that we are not exposed to actual places and stories involving the many religious people throughout the ages.

On the Camino, for a few weeks of your life, you give up all the luxuries and comforts you normally surround yourself with daily and immerse yourself in a spiritual and physically challenging journey. Each day you head to a new destination, not knowing where you are going to put your head down at the end of the day. You meet all sorts of people from all parts of the world undertaking the pilgrimage for their own reasons. Your share meals with fellow pilgrims who gladly share their life experiences with complete strangers. Your only link is that you had all decided to experience the real meaning of life, missing in the hustle and bustle of daily living.

Each morning you step out of your normal daily routine in exchange for life on the road. Your legs protest, your backpack seems heavier and yet you look forward to contemplating the deeper issues of life and its meaning. You have many hours to look at your relationship with God. You recall your relationships with family members alive and those passed on. After a few days you are able to focus more and more on real issues and discard all the little things you tend to clutter up your mind with.

You are able to spend quality time with God. You ponder on the reason why you are here on earth. In the ensuing days, your faith is nurtured, grown and strengthened.

The gift of complete freedom from daily routine back home is indeed a wonderful and refreshing experience. You leave behind the worries of having to give constant attention to issues, which is exhausting and energy-sapping. Even the little niggling matters which require your daily attention suddenly don't really require your attention anymore. Most pilgrims make a conscious decision to step away for their normal lives in a search for something which is physically challenging to find an inner peace of mind as they contemplate the deeper issues of life.

Returning home, you are a changed person. It is not that walking the Camino is a life-changing experience but rather you have a greater appreciation of the many things you ordinarily would not have noticed or even appreciated. The little things you just take for granted now assume a greater significance and enrich your life.

Personally, you develop a more meaningful relationship with God as you contemplate the future and truly understand God's plan for your life. You feel an incredible peace fall on you as you forge ahead each day. You listen to the clear, simple and personal messages as you take time off from your worldly worries and listen to God.

In September 2011 Lynne and I and our parish priest Fr John Finlayson ambitiously walked our first Camino – the Camino Frances, the most popular of all the Camino routes from Pamplona to Santiago, a distance of 800 km, in 35 days, followed two years later by the Portuguese Camino from Porto to Santiago, about 235 km in 23 days and our latest pilgrimage took place in September 2017, known as '*Via Podensis*', when we planned to walk from Le Puy in France to St Jean Pied de Port, a beautiful bustling French market town in the foothills of the Pyrenees, then cross over into Spain following tracks used by shepherds and pilgrims for centuries to finish in Pamplona, known for the fiesta of San Fermin, made famous by the American writer Ernest Hemingway in his masterpiece *The Running of the Bulls*.

But this last Camino, also known as Chemin de Compostelle, did not go as planned. Fr John was 82, Lynne 73 and myself 78. We had to contend with bad weather during the first half, which we largely avoided by catching taxis, buses and trains. The terrain was very slippery in the wet weather, the mountains were stamina sapping and frankly, I was too ambitious in thinking we could walk anything from 15 km to 30 km per day, continuously for 40 days. We walked from five hours to seven hours each day, which was what we could manage without being too physically exhausted at the end of each day because we had to still find our accommodation, shower and visit places of interest. Towards the end of our pilgrimage, we found that some of small hotels or hostels (known as *gites*) had closed for the season, leaving the distances between the remaining accommodations too much to cover in a single day. But still, we can be proud of what we did, in fact, achieve - about340 km - in the available time, a far cry from the planned 800 km.

Nevertheless, it was a wonderful experience of physical endurance, battling with the French language, learning about the early history of France, visiting churches and attending Masses, swapping experiences with fellow pilgrims and seeing how the different local regions lived out their daily lives.

We have a deep admiration for the many pilgrims who for many varied reasons undertake the pilgrimage - seeking a new direction in life, grieving the loss of a loved one, losing a job, searching for new meaning in their life. In some cases we could only marvel at the distances pilgrims of all ages from places like Sweden, Germany and Italy had planned to walk from their home base to join the Chemin de Compostelle from Le Puy to St Jean Pied de Port, over the Pyrenees mountains to Pamplona to join the Compostelle Frances to Santiago – a staggering 1 600 km in two to three months!

We leave it to future generation to finish what we did not manage - reaching St Jean Pied de Port and crossing the Pyrenees Mountains. Maybe, just maybe, we might take up the challenge again next year and start where we finished off in 2017 and tackle the remaining 126km which we were forced to abandon because of time constraints, remaining distances and physical exhaustion.

To get a greater appreciation of what is involved in a pilgrimage, there are a number of films to watch and useful books to read to get more information about this life-changing experience. A wonderful and humorous movie to watch is called *The Way* with Martin Sheen starring.

On the Camino you take a journey into the past, visiting beautiful churches and medieval villages, experiencing local cuisine, local traditions and customs and meeting fellow pilgrims, hearing their stories and gaining an appreciation of the daily problems which people the world over have to face. You realise that nowhere in the world is life easier than back home. You appreciate returning home a much wiser person.

Modern pilgrims choose the numerous routes all over Europe for the personal, spiritual or physical challenge - to walk or cycle and take time out from their busy modern lives. Whatever their reasons for undertaking the pilgrimages many become addicted, as they enjoy meeting fellow pilgrims, sharing experiences or gaining spiritual insights.

If asked what I benefited from undertaking the various Caminos - was it to deepen my understanding of God, was it the physical challenge, was it the spiritual experience, was it meeting pilgrims, was it sharing experiences, was it to be a role model to family, was it simply to move out of my comfort zone? - in all honesty, I would have to admit I don't really know.

Perhaps, in the final analysis, it is the realisation that each one of us must try to live life to the fullest. To live your life without having an achievable goal ahead, no matter how small or big is detrimental to your mental state, physical well-being and ultimate enjoyment.

Maybe my real objective was to encourage people to take control of their lives, no matter how difficult the circumstances. The smallest conscious effort each day is very necessary and beneficial to a person's daily wellbeing. This could be as simple as on waking up each morning to look in the mirror and force a smile. Just remember that a scowl or an unhappy face puts off the people you come across in your day. Then set your sights as you plan your day - phone a friend who would appreciate your concern, do something to help someone less fortunate than yourself, undertake meaningful interaction with somebody in need, take a genuine interest in the world at large, so you are able to converse with others and give your input to make a better world.

One of my lasting memories and a constant reminder of what I learned from these pilgrimages is struggling up the Valance Valley up to O'Cebreiro in Galicia in Spain in swirling mist to find a rain-sodden, handwritten poem pinned on a closed church door at La Faba. I was so impressed with the poem that after we returned home I searched the Internet for the words:

Prayer of La Faba

Although I may have travelled all the roads,
Crossed mountains and valleys from East to West,
If I have not discovered the freedom to be myself,
I have arrived nowhere.
Although I may have shared all my possessions
with people of other languages and cultures
made friends with Pilgrims of a thousand paths,
or shared an albergue with saints and princes,
if I am not capable of forgiving my neighbour tomorrow,

I am determined in my remaining years to lead a gainful and useful existence and not to be a burden on our families. Another reason is that we older persons must accept our responsibility of being role models for upcoming generations on how to live meaningful lives, always be available to talk to when someone needs a sympathetic ear just to listen quietly or offer a sympathetic shoulder to cry on, not be a coward or frightened to speak out firmly when clearly strong action is required, give sound advice or to counsel, as these are troubled times we live in. Such unselfish action at no cost will be greatly appreciated.

Funny how you think your life just goes on normally as the years go by and you are still in full control as in the past. But, in reality, an older person's personality and physical abilities change, dramatically or slowly, according to how you have lived your life or the genes you inherited from those who have passed on. Yes, you change a lot in ways you are simply not fully aware of – more cantankerous, more difficult to accept other viewpoints, more stubborn and more slow-moving, which is frustrating and irritating to younger people. The warning signs are clearly seen by others and, if you are not careful, not necessarily by yourself.

My personal view is that older people, especially grandparents, must live on their own for as long as financially possible and only then, if necessary, to move into a retirement village for companionship and medical assistance. This comes at a price, as living with other older people pulls you down to their level and definitely ages you if you are still mentally and physically active. So, if you want to lead a peaceful and trouble-free existence in retirement, do not move in with family under the same roof! Keep yourself busy and be in touch with the world around you and yes, participate in as many family and community functions as possible, but value your independence.

We definitely experienced the reality of advancing years and felt the effects of growing older when we when tackled our third and definitely last Camino - Chemin from Le Puy in mid-France to Pamplona in Northern Spain in September 2017. I must confess with hindsight that it was an over-ambitious plan to start with. When Fr John Finlayson retired as our parish priest at St Joseph in Primrose in September 2016, I suggested to him that we meet at Charles de Gaulle airport in France in a year's time to undertake the ancient pilgrimage in France. It is always important in life to have some target to aim for in the future, no matter how ambitious or unrealistic, in order to concentrate your mind, have a reason to live, instead of merely going through the daily motions of living and making a nuisance of yourself, dragging everybody down with your own self-pity and coping with ever-growing ailments and rows of pills and medication.

I must admit I am at a crossroads in my life at this point in time. Lynne and I recently returned after a three month trip overseas, where we visited Trevor, Leah-Marie, Nicholas and Julia in New Jersey, visited Lourdes for a deacon's conference, spent time in Paris, walked part of the Chemin de Compostelle in France in September and October with our former parish priest Fr John Finlayson. From there we stayed with Kevin and Gill and their family in Dorridge in the UK and celebrated my 78th birthday with Jessica and Thomas, enjoying a meal in Birmingham. We spent a few days sightseeing in London and met up with Graeme and Donovan before finally flying back to South Africa to decide how to occupy my time.

Now I must put into practice what I have recorded in this book, about keeping busy in retirement and find meaningful things to do and enjoy life to the fullest with family and friends. And, if at all possible, leave a legacy for future generations.

Looking After Planet Earth

There is another important goal that I have set myself in my retirement.

It is the care of the environment and our collective responsibility to care for the world, our common home. This is a challenge for the entire human race as we must tackle pollution, climate change, scarcity of water, loss of biodiversity and the decline of the quality of human life. We must close the growing gap between the haves and the have nots of this world, helping with the chronic unemployment in the country and, most importantly, promoting the values of family life.

I make no apologies for quoting Pope Francis again, one of the few real leaders in the world who is genuinely concerned about our responsibility to care for the world, our common home, unlike many leaders in the world who put national interests first. In his encyclical *Laudato Si'* (Praise be to you), a name borrowed from St Francis of Assisi, who is described in the document as the example par excellence of care for the vulnerable and of an integral ecology lived out joyfully and authentically. The pope recalls the words of St Francis that the earth is our sister who cries out to us to acknowledge our sins. We are not her masters, we are partners. As we sin against creation we sin against ourselves and against God. Environmental or ecological education is for everyone and includes a sense of the spiritual, not only the material. The question is, what will it cost? This is not only a financial issue but a moral and relational one too. Countries cannot ignore the challenges of narrow self-interest and neither can communities at any level.

Laudato Si' is taken from the invocation of the Canticle of the Creatures. In the words of this beautiful canticle, St Francis of Assisi reminds us that our common home is like a sister with whom we share our life and a beautiful mother who opens her arms to embrace us. *Praise be to you, my Lord, through our Sister, Mother Earth, who sustains and governs us, and who produces various fruit with coloured flowers and herbs.*

The need for change in lifestyle is explained in paragraph 225 of *Laudato Si',* which resonates with me as I look ahead and plan to be involved in a shared communal work for the ecology:

Inner peace is closely related to care for ecology and for the common good because, lived out authentically, it is reflected in a balanced lifestyle, together with a capacity for wonder which takes us to a deeper understanding of life. Nature is filled with words of love, but how can we listen to them amid constant noise, interminable and nerve-wracking distractions or the cult of appearances? Many sense a profound imbalance..... An integral ecology includes taking time to recover a serene harmony with creation, reflecting on our lifestyle and our ideals, and contemplating the Creator who lives among us and surrounds us, whose presence must not be contrived but found, uncovered.

It seems perfectly logical to me after contemplating the future direction of my life in retirement that the methodology of Liberation Theology of **See, Judge and Act** and of getting involved in the ecology will give me a sense of purpose and satisfaction.

What about laying out footpaths on Linksfield Ridge from Gillooly's Farm to Sylvia's Pass so that families can get together to enjoy walks and hikes and view the scenery?

It is with some anticipation but great trepidation that I contemplate the huge but exciting challenges ahead: walking the talk; mapping out the paths; working with the Johannesburg and

Ekurhuleni councils with all their red tape, getting unemployed youth involved in the physical work of laying of stones extracted from the proposed second water reservoir; soliciting cash donations and sponsorships from businesses for equipment; material and labour; harnessing professional skills from universities, construction firms and voluntary organisations such as hiking clubs, schools and environmental groups to undertake specific projects and involving the community and likeminded people to develop and save our little corner of the planet for future generations.

It is for this reason that I established **The Douglas Boake Foundation** - to coordinate all my future efforts and energies for the care for our common home on earth.

A vivid picture is painted in an article titled *A World to Live in: On Being a Catholic Architect* by David H Armitage, in *Professions of Faith*, edited by James Martin SJ and Jeremy Langford, on the initial physical creation of the world and the role we are expected to play to continue God's creation to create a safe place for families to appreciate the wonders of nature and enjoy life:

The story of Genesis, with God's creation of the world, describes the coming of light into the darkness. Since childhood, I have found the image of God as architect of the universe immensely compelling. Medieval images of God, the architect and, more recently, William Blake's powerful depiction of God the architect remain for me critical images of who God is. Few images show God so at work, so human, as these images.

The images depict God thinking, physically active, striding, measuring, and contemplating. The writer of Genesis tells us that after each day's work God paused and saw 'that it was good', and on the seventh day, God rested from his labours. We have before us in Genesis the first example of the contemplative person in action and of the active person contemplating.

Embedded in the story of the creation of the world is the story of the creation of every building. From a formless mass emerges something habitable, beautifully decorated, and safe. The story of creation and of the construction of the world informs my own understanding of the purpose of all buildings: a shelter from whatever threatens, as a dwelling place, as a home.

The Our Father tells us 'Thy kingdom come, thy will be done, on earth, as it is in heaven'.

All human beings, as children of God, are called to participate in God's ongoing creation of order out of disorder. We are called to create a world of love and compassion out of a world that is often chaotic and threatening. In a world full of distractions, it is easy to lose sight of this. But, I have found, the experiences that have emerged out of my faith life help me to stay focused, to stay the course and to maintain the sight of the mission.

Yes, this seems to be a wonderful project to start in my looming retirement to continue with God's creation of our world. The least I can do to make a start with the grand plan and others can then take over for the benefit of the present and future generations.

I am inspired in my future endeavours by the words of this powerful pray given by Pope Francis in Rome at St Peter's on 24 May, the Solemnity of Pentecost, in 2015, the third year of his Pontificate.

> *Father, we praise you with all your creatures.*
> *They came forth from your all-powerful hand;*
> *They are yours, filled with your presence and your tender love.*
> *Praise be to you!*
> *Son of God, Jesus, through you all things were made.*
> *You were formed in the womb of Mary our Mother,*
> *you became part of this earth,*
> *you became part of this earth,*
> *and you gazed upon this world with human eyes.*
> *Today you are alive in every creature*
> *in your risen glory.*
> *Praise to you!*
> *Holy Spirit, by your light*
> *you guide this world towards the Father's love*
> *and accompany creation as it groans in travail.*
> *You also dwell in our hearts*
> *and you inspire us to do what is good.*

Praise be to you!
Triune Lord, wondrous community of infinite love,
teach us to contemplate you
in the beauty of the universe,
for all things speak of you.
Awaken our praise and thankfulness
for every being that you have made.
Give us the grace to feel profoundly joined
to everything that is.
God of love, show us our place in this world
as channels of your love
for all creatures of this earth,
for not one of them is forgotten in your sight.
Enlighten those who possess power and money
that that they may love the common good, advance the weak,
that they may avoid the sin of indifference,
and care for this world in which we live.
The poor and the earth are crying out.
O Lord, seize us with your power and light,
help us to protect all life,
to prepare for a better future,
for the coming of your Kingdom
of justice, peace, love and beauty.
Praise be to you!
Amen.

Chapter 7
Facing The End

Our Ache for Earthly Immortality

As I grow older I find myself more and more removed, not by choice, from the mainstream of my past life – family work, friends and sport – understandably so, as one physically slows down although mentally you think you can keep up, but every now and then, you notice forgetfulness, new aches and pains and a lack of mobility and co-ordination. Getting older is not for the faint-hearted as it is new unchartered territory that in your twilight years you are entering with some trepidation.

Without sounding too morbid I found that I am spending more time nowadays looking back at my humble, ordinary life, shared with billions of others, and appreciating a sense of the preciousness, meaning and significance of life.

I recently read an article by Ron Rolheiser OMI titled *Our Ache for Earthly Immortality* which expresses my sentiments about this subject and which I share with you:

Thomas Merton, a Trappist monk, on one of his less restless days, said: "It is enough to be, in an ordinary human code, with one's hunger and sleep, one's cold and warmth, rising and going to bed. Putting on blankets and taking them off, making coffee and then drinking it. Defrosting the refrigerator, reading, meditating, working and praying. I live as my fathers have lived on this earth, until eventually I die. Amen"'.

We share the world with more than seven and half billion people and each of us has the irrepressible, innate sense that we are special and uniquely destined. This isn't surprising since each one of us is indeed unique and special. But how does one feel special among seven and a half billion others?

We try to stand out. Generally we don't succeed and so, as Allan Jones puts it: We nurse within our hearts the hope that we are different, that we are special, that we are extraordinary.

Few things impede our peace and happiness as does this effort. We set ourselves the impossible, frustrating task of assuring for ourselves something which only God can give us, significance and immortality.

Ordinary life then never seems enough for us, and we live restless, competitive, driven lives. Why isn't ordinary life enough for us? Why do our lives always seem too small and not exciting enough? Why do we habitually feel dissatisfied at not being special?

Why our need to leave a mark? Why does our own situation often feel so suffocating?

Why can't we more easily embrace each other as sisters and brothers, and rejoice in each other's gifts and each other's existence? Why the perennial feeling that the other is a rival?

Why the need for masks, for presence, to project a certain image about ourselves?

The answer: We do all these things to try to set ourselves apart because we are trying to give ourselves something that only God can give us: significance and immortality.

Scripture tells us that faith alone saves. That simple line reveals the secret: Only God gives eternal life. Preciousness, meaning, significance and immortality are free gifts from God and we would be a whole lot more restful, humble, grateful, happy and less competitive if we could believe that.

Journey of the Spirit

The poem *Journey of the Spirit* by Morton Kersley was written as he sat in silent communion at the bedside of his dying son. I am sure that these words are inspiring and will give comfort to grieving Christian families as its message is one of infinite hope of eternal life through the resurrection of Jesus.

> *Fear not for me. I am not afraid.*
> *A new adventure awaits me,*
> *A new, more brilliant being*
> *is about to birth*

into a different place and time.
The garden of heaven and those abiding there
are calling me insistently.
They want me soon.
They sing of my courage and frustration,
Of years of seeking, restless searching.....
So many roads have petered out
in scorching desert and burning sand
and still I kept on, was guided.
Those voices promise
to answer all my questions
with love abounded, limitless.
They offer intimacy, closeness, far richer
than I had dared to hope for, and wisdom, too.
And living waters drawn from the deepest wells
that holds the secret mysteries safe
from vain and curious wanderers.
The voices also sing of love and loving,
of giving all I had and only at this moment
knowing that my arrow struck its mark.
Do not hold me back. I'll be with you still
in fuller measure than I've ever been before.
The sun is rising from the sea
as one by one the stars are lost in light.
The broken has been mended.
I can be loved and love.
It is time to go
pushed beyond the limits
of death and pain and hope
I find the real, Eternal life.
Amen.

Memories

Looking back on the highs and lows in my life, I have no regrets because I have enjoyed the great moments and also accepted the challenges. Each one of us only has one life to live. So I have lived my life to the fullest and enjoyed the journey.

The apostle St Paul wrote in 2 Timothy 4:7 these memorable words near the end of his life as he reflected on his own victories and struggle:

As for me, I am already being poured out in libation, and the time of my departure has come. I have fought the good fight, I have finished the race, I have kept the faith. From now on there is reserved for me the crown of righteousness, which the Lord, the righteous judge, will give me on that day, and not only to me but to all who have longed for His appearing.

I can relate to his feelings as I have tried my best with varying degrees of success in all situations and that, after all, is what really matters.

I look back with fond memories – a happy marriage, family, friends, Comrades Marathon aches and pain, which has proven to be glue for the family and a yardstick for those brave enough to have taken part in it and for its sheer enjoyment and competitiveness, Caminos - especially as we had to face the reality of getting on in years - the mental anguish of the criminal trial and the civil action which lasted for more than 10 years and the sheer joy and relief when we were finally found not guilty, and the numerous other special small moments with family and friends taken to enjoy and appreciate life over the years.

Role Model

I have always felt a deep responsibility to be a role model for our wonderful family, getting involved in each one's wellbeing, passing on practical insights, writing three books – '*My Journey*', '*Goodbye Debbie*' and '*Of Family and Faith*'), my humble efforts in serving Christ in daily life, being a member of the Board of Governors of St Benedict's College, a Catholic School for Boys, for 18 years, community service through Bedfordview Round Table, Hillbrow Rotary Club (recognised with a Paul Harris Award) and Little Eden (honoured with The Domitilla and Danny Hyam's Award for 40 years' service as treasurer) and as a deacon at St Joseph Catholic Parish in Primrose since 2011.

We all can recall an event, a saying or something in our lives which we vividly recall as an important milestone, a shining beacon or a significant influence on our thinking or which shaped our lives thereafter. Most times, it simply passed by at the time but later, chances are many years later, you suddenly realise its importance. I simply have many happy memories.

We live in a terrible modern world simply spinning out of control with very little quality time to spend together as a family, be it at a meal, outings or special functions. All too often we only realise years later when it is too late. So it is worthwhile, whatever the cost or difficulties or inconveniences, to plan to spend special time together to bond the family ties and create happy memories.

We can all tell stories of personal experiences where this happened in our own family circle or with close friends.

As parents of four boys, we were always involved with them in their growing-up years. We never expected them to be called on stage at the prize-giving for academic awards, but we were pleasantly surprised from time to time. The boys were more sports-focused and excelled in all the different sports offered at school - soccer, tennis, cricket and athletics. We believe that active participation in sport helps in the all-round development of youngsters, as it is competitive, assists in mastering body skills and co-ordination, learning to accept good and bad results with good grace and forms the basis of life-long friendships. Also, participation in sport kept them busy outdoors and away from other distractions such as parties, social media and keeping bad company.

I remember many years ago when Lynne and I attended a prize-giving for our youngest son Trevor in primary school. The headmaster Duncan Fredericks, who was an orphan from a very young age, read out a poem to the assembly of boys and parents. You could sense his personal pain at what he had lost out on when growing up without close family. The words of this tear-jerker forcefully brought home to the audience the need to do things together as a family and face whatever challenges have to be confronted as a family – believe me they will come fast and furious. Sadly this is a problem today with so many families breaking up and parents separated or torn between the stresses of work and family life.

This, in fact, is one of my reasons for writing this book - to help families recognise the issues and suggesting ways to try and tackle those issues.

Written in 1974, this song topped the hit parade for a long time. It's about a father who is too busy to spend time with his son, an all too familiar scene nowadays. In the end, the grown-up son is too busy for his elderly father. The fact that composer Harry Chaplin died in a car accident in 1981 and never got to see his own children grow up, made the song somehow even sadder.

Cat's In The Cradle

My child arrived just the other day.
He came to the world in the usual way.
But there were planes to catch, and bills to pay.
He learned to walk whilst I was away,
And he was talking 'fore I knew it, and as he grew
He'd say "I gonna be like you, dad
You know I 'm gonna be like you."
    And the cat's in the cradle and the silver spoon
    Little boy blue and the man on the moon
    "When you comin' home, dad?
    "I don't know when, but we will get together then.
    You know we'll have a good time then".
My son turned ten the other day.
He said, "Thanks for the ball, Dad, come and play.
Can you teach me to throw"? I said "Not today.
I got a lot to do". He said "That's OK"
And walked away but his smile never dimmed
And said "I'm gonna be like him. Yeah.
You know I am gonna be like him."
    And the cat's in the cradle and the silver spoon
    Little boy blue and the man on the moon.
    "When you comin' home, Dad?"
    "I don't know when, but we'll get together then.
    You know we'll have a good time then."
Well, he came from college just the other day.
So much like a man I just had to say.
"Son, I am proud of you, can you sit a while?"
"What I'd really like, Dad, is to borrow the car keys.
See you later, can I have them please?"

And the cat's in the cradle and the silver spoon
Little boy blue and the man on the moon
"When you comin' home son?"
"I don't know when, but we'll get together then, Dad.
You know we'll have a good time then."
I've long since retired. My son has moved away.
I called him just the other day.
I said ""I like to see you if you don't mind."
He said. "I'd love to, Dad, if I can find the time.
You see my new job's a hassle and the kids have the flu.
But it's sure nice talking to you, Dad.
It's been sure nice talking to you."
And as I hung up the phone it occurred to me.
He'd grown up just like me.
My boy was just like me.

Cat's in the Cradle brings generations together. In shuddering sobs.

The following article by Robyn Passante which appeared in *The Washington Post* on 7th February 2017 brings home the reality of the important role and presence of both parents in the home, especially for younger children. I searched for some clue whether there was a father in the home, either deceased or divorced, as sadly I suspect that this is a single mother trying to bring up the family alone and the children are longing to relate to their absent father.

This is what she wrote with real feelings:

I try to accomplish two things at the dinner table. The first is to get at a portion of the healthy, balanced meal I've put on the table into my two son's bodies. The second is to polish their table manners. This mostly involves telling them to stop jumping up from their seats like jacks-in-the-box, bargaining with them over "how many more bites" and attempting to engage them in some sort of civil discussion.

It often feels like we are worlds apart, even when we are at the same table. My world has Brussels sprouts, chilled chardonnay and polite dinner conversation; theirs has bathroom humour and ketchup. A lot of ketchup. But once in a while, dinner talk turns to something that reminds me of our similarities rather than our differences. Recently that "something" was a pang of sadness universally felt on hearing Harry Chaplin's most famous song.

My fourth-grader, Kostyn, was telling us he had music class that morning, and his teacher made them sing a song he had never heard. I asked what it was and he said he didn't know the title.

"It's about a little boy and a dad and the boy grows up and comes back home," he said. Then he began singing a snippet he remembered: "Little boy blue and the man in the moon."

"Huh. He's teaching you "Cat's in the Cradle?" I asked, a little bewildered given the substance of the song.

But Kostyn was no longer singing. He was staring at an invisible point above the table, his little chin quivering. Then his eyes closed, and the floodgates opened. Tears streamed down his cheeks as he began to sob.

"It's just soooo saaaad", he said, his whole upper body shuddering. Nodding knowingly, I reached out and pulled him toward me as his little brother looked wide-eyed at us from across the table.

My 9-year-old was understandably inconsolable over Chapin's folk hit from the '70s, blubbering between cries about what a tragically sad song it is and saying that he doesn't want to grow up. Like, ever.

As I cradled his not-quite-big-boy body in my arms, I had a flash of a memory: Me, at age 12 or 13, sitting in my dad's silvery blue Mazda pickup truck driving somewhere with him when that song comes on the radio. I can smell the scent of Dad's pipe tobacco and see the clutter of drafting papers and mechanical pencils on the seat between us as I listen to the lyrics.   My chin quivers and I steal a glance at my father, whose eyes are welled with tears too. I lose it then, overwhelmed with love for my dad and the ache that comes with knowing that it all goes too fast, that we only get one shot.

Curse you, Harry.

I pushed the memory to the recesses of my mind and wiped away my own tears, then offered Kostyn my napkin to wipe his. The baked chicken and biscuits sat cooling on our plates; my 7-year-old took tentative bites of his cantaloupe, not understanding what the heck was happening on the other side of the table.

"Every time we sang the song I had this memory, one of my favourite memories, of me and Evan and Dad playing a game at sunset," Kostyn said, sniffing, "only now in my mind I'm all grown up in the memory and I can't play anymore, and it's all wrong!"

I remember being his age and wanting to remain a kid forever, having absolutely no inkling of all the good grown-up things to come. I tried to explain to his rattled heart how childhood is a journey that lasts years and years, and how he's still going to be young for a long time.

"I know it doesn't seem like it now, but someday you're going to want to get older, to do things like drive a car and stay up late", I said, my voice breaking at the thought. "But there is no rush."

And then, because I got a little too excited about us being on the same wavelength, I took things one step further.

"You know the real reason that the song is sad?" I asked, pulling up the lyrics on my phone and reading them, line by line, to two hesitantly curious boys. When I finished, and the singer had hung up the phone in his song, nobody at the table looked any happier. But I pressed on.

"See, it's not just about growing up, it's about regret," I explained. "It's about being too busy for each other and taking each other for granted." My voice was cracking again, which Kostyn noticed. "And we don't do that. We spend a lot of time together. You said one of your favourite memories is of you and Daddy at sunset, right?"

"I guess, yeah," he said, sliding off my lap and back to his seat.

Finally, as I reheated his chicken, we talked about the power of music to make you feel something you maybe haven't even actually experienced in real life.

"When you think about it, it is really a great song in that way," I said.

"Well," Kostyn said, defiance rising up, "if my teacher tries to make us sing it again, I'm going to tell him to stop picking sad songs. I don't have to sing it, right?"

"I think you absolutely should tell him that," I said with a smile, realising that despite all the tears, this nearly 40-year-old tune had helped to produce polite dinner conversation and the motivation for a young boy to speak his mind.

Thank you, Harry.

My plea to all parents is not to let this happen to your family, to avoid the very sad consequences later on.

Grateful for Professional Achievements

There is also the satisfaction on my part of establishing Boake Inc, a professional firm of auditors and accountants in Bedfordview, which is more than 50 years old and continues to grow from strength to strength. Graeme accepted an award on behalf of Boake Inc in recognition and appreciation for the firm's 20 years of dedicated membership and superior client service from BKR International, which is a worldwide association of independent accounting and business advisory firms, at the World Conference held in London in October 2017.

In Post-Apartheid South Africa from 1994 politicians seem hell-bent on stirring racial tensions among all race groups for their own narrow political agendas. Boake Inc is proud of our UBUNTU achievements which are aimed at the promotion of peace, security and development of staff, clients and community. UBUNTU is an African idea of personhood: persons depend on other persons to be.

We believe all peoples of South Africa must mobilise the concept of UBUNTU so as to tackle the range of serious issues that confront our country in order to attain the status of a Rainbow Nation.

Bits And Pieces – An Old Accountant Recalls The Past

This was my talk at the BKR Africa Sub Region meeting held in Pretoria in March 2018, when I was invited to share with the delegates some of my personal experiences in public practice, spanning more than half a century.

I was touched as after the talk the wife of our Nigerian member asked me for my notes as she intended to use my practical experiences in her presentations to businessmen and government back home.

Around drinks afterwards, all the delegates from Africa told horrifying stories of corruption and dishonesty in their countries. At least we from South Africa did not feel we were alone in fighting State Capture, abuses by the ruling party, government and businesses.

This is what I said to the delegates:

I am humbled that Heinrich has asked me to address you today.

Let me start with a lovely poem from Mary Oliver:

> *"When it's all over I don't want to wonder*
> *if I have made of my life something particular, and real.*
> *I don't want to find myself sighing*
> *and frightened or full of argument.*
> *I don't want to end up simply having visited this world."*

The best advice I can offer you is to accept the changes, welcome the future and learn to laugh with the world and at yourself.

The world is certainly changing and changing so fast that the older generation – everybody over 25 - better sit up and listen and take note and assess their own priorities in a new world at home, at work, family relationships, personal wealth and health.

To my way of thinking parents and society in general have lost their way and as a result children and the younger generation today are searching.

I am so concerned that I am writing a book in which I will explore two critical areas which will be the title of my book – "Of Family and Faith".

I have been around for a little while – I was born in 1939 at the start of World War 2.

I served articles from 1958 to 1963 and qualified as a Chartered Accountant in 1964.

I wrote the final Board Exam twice - the first time the pass rate was 39% - I failed. The next year the pass mark was 40% - I passed.

At the age of 25 in 1964, I became a 50% partner in the practice Pittman & Boake so I have been in public practice for 54 years.

So what have I learned?

The famous Italian poet Dante wrote "The Divine Comedy" at the age of 35 – midlife by biblical reckoning. The measure of our life is three score and ten which means 70 (Psalm 90:10).

He realised "midway on the journey of my life, I wake to find myself in a dark wood, having wandered from the straight path. He woke up to it."

To use his metaphor "was a signal virtue and the impetus for his journey", uch as "hitting bottom" and "turning one life's over to a Higher Power", are essential for those who undertake the 12 steps.

Don't ask me what these 12 steps are. Maybe if I can remember, I will let you know next year!

Many years ago Lynne and I attended a BKR conference in Las Vegas. The keynote speaker was the Chairman of the CPA'S in the USA and he was also the Chairman of the New York Stock Exchange at the same time. He spoke about the regulations of the profession.

He claimed that as long as the auditor complied strictly with the laid-down rules of the profession, the auditor was OK – no blame could be pinned on him.

What he forgot to say that at all times simple common sense must prevail and you must follow your gut instincts - if it looks fishy it is fishy.

So there is a problem.

Within a year the Enron scandal broke in the States - one of the world's greatest fraud cases which resulted in the collapse of the world's largest auditing firm. Arthur Anderson was closed down within one year.

Ironically Arthur Anderson was found not guilty a few years later, but by then it was too late.

The chairman of Enron had committed suicide and his financial accountant went to gaol for twenty years.

Lesson to be learnt: Size does not matter.

What is more important are Ethics and Morality and Good Governance.

Another lesson: Bad publicity, no matter whether wrong or right, has serious consequences for the reputation of a professional firm.

So we move to South Africa.

KPMG, one of the Big Four auditing firms, was involved in the Gupta State Capture saga.

With all the modern audit techniques and procedures and layers of reviews, how could this have happened on such a large scale?

I read somewhere that a junior audit clerk in the firm raised the alarm bells when he queried the payment of R30 million for the Guptas' wedding at Sun City out of the Vrede farming operations!

There must have been major collusion between all parties to hide this.

The lesson to be learnt: Greed is very common today.

There are serious consequences if you are drawn in or involved. It is not worth it.

Make a stand and take appropriate action to safeguard yourself. You studied hard for your qualification so guard it jealously.

Even closer home at Boake Incorporated, Graeme and I were charged in criminal and civil actions for simply signing two audit certificates to support loan applications to the Industrial Development Corporation on behalf of a client.

The lesson to be learnt: That even if you do everything according to laid-down auditing standards, the rest of the world sees things differently to suit their case against you - public prosecutors, attorneys, advocates, magistrates, judges, the Scorpions, the Hawks, the Industrial Development Corporation.

It took us 10 years and 42 court appearances to be found "not guilty" of fraud, corruption and money laundering by the Special Commercial Crimes Court (Case SCCA 208/11) on 13th December 2013 and the civil case against us was dismissed with costs by the Supreme Court of Appeal in Bloemfontein (Motala v The Master 313/13ZASCA 185 29th November 2013).

Lesson to be learnt: We live in a hostile and litigious business environment so it is important to be extremely vigilant, exercise special care, be sceptical and trust no one and make sure all your documentation is supportive of your actions.

I could not keep from smiling when I read about the recent merging of the audit practices of Grant Thornton and Sizwe Gobodo, clearly to challenge the dominance of the BIG FOUR audit firms.

In our case, the evidence in the report by Gobodo was the assertion by a junior audit clerk of that firm that fraud had been committed because she looked at the bank statements and she couldn't find any manufacturing plant deposited into the bank account!

I read in the Business Day this morning that the investigators into the debacle at Steinhoff International found two cheques made out at year-end -the first cheque of R100 million was debited to cost of sales and the second cheque for R30 million was debited to reduce the interest charge.

Lesson to be learnt: Check carefully the work of your staff and, if not up to the required standard, then follow the example of Donald Trump, the recent USA president:

"You're FIRED".

Now on a less serious note:

Life is for living and this is only possible if you take care of your health, if you exercise regularly, drink moderately, be weight conscious, eat sensibly, stop smoking, get adequate sleep and get rid of stress.

Lynne and I have undertaken three pilgrimages:

2011 Camino Frances – Pamplona to Santiago (800 km)

2013 Portuguese Camino – Porto to Santiago (241km)

2017 Chemin de Compostelle – Le Puy to Arzacq- Arraziguet (314 km) and in September 2018 we plan to plan to walk to complete our walk from Arzacq-Arraziguet over the Pyreness Mountains to Pamplona (186 km).

The most important quality in life should be the ability to laugh.

In her book, 300 Questions Couples should ask before Marriage, Shannon L Alder penned these words which captures the realities of life facing each one of us:

Beauty fades, careers end, money comes and goes, religion changes, children grow up and move away, spouses get sick, struggles happen, family members die, senility sets in when you older, but the ability to have a sense of humour every day is the most precious gift God can give you to get through it all.

I found this poem for older folks like myself in a shop window in Port Alfred and wonder if this is what I can look forward to in the years ahead:

> *A row of bottles on my shelf*
> *cause me to analyse myself.*
> *One yellow pill I have to pop*
> *goes to my heart so it won't stop.*

A little one that I take
goes to my hands so they won't shake.
The blue ones that I use a lot
tell me I'm happy when I am not.
The purple pill goes to my brain
and tells me that I have no pain.
The capsules tell me not to wheeze
or cough or choke or even sneeze.
The red ones, smallest of them all
go to my blood so I won't fall.
The orange ones, big and bright
prevent my leg cramps at night.
Such an array of brilliant pills
helping to cure all kinds of ills,
But what I'd really like to know
is what tells them where to go!

Walk the Talk

Our world is in a real mess and we are not going to fix it without a new approach and a different mindset, otherwise, each of us will continue to contribute to the chaos.

My purpose in writing this book arose from my personal need to examine my own beliefs.

Also, I wanted to look at the present problems facing my immediate family, other families and the expected problems which future generations will have to contend with.

It gradually dawned on me that the fundamental problem to be addressed was the important role of a stable family unit and the glue that keeps members together – the faith they practice.

Whatever our individual experiences are and wherever our journey leads us, we must be open to new challenges and, from time to time, we need some space and time to reflect on the purpose of life.

These words immortalised in Nelson's Mandela's Freedom Speech remind us of our true identity:

Our deepest fear is not that we are inadequate.

Our deepest fear is that we are powerful beyond measure.

It is our Light, not our Darkness, that frightens us.

We ask ourselves, who am I to be brilliant, gorgeous, talented and fabulous?

Actually, who you are not to be?

You are a child of God.

Your playing small doesn't serve the world.

There's nothing enlightening about shrinking so that other people

won't feel insecure around you.

We are born to manifest the Glory of God that is within us.

It's not just in some of us; it's in everyone.

And as we let our Light shine, we unconsciously give other people

* permission to do the same.*

As we are liberated from our fear, our presence automatically liberates others.

Temporary Crown

It is important to reflect on the words of St Paul in 1 Cor 9:25 as a constant reminder of our purpose here on earth: *However we run not for a temporary crown, but for an eternal one.*

* * *

Final Prayer

This prayer explains beautifully and simply the key goals what we should strive for in living our daily lives:

> *Lord, grant us simplicity of faith,*
>
> *and a generosity of service*
>
> *that gives without counting the cost:*
>
> *a life overflowing with Grace poured out,*
>
> *from the One who gave everything,*
>
> *that we might show the power of love*
>
> *to a broken world*
>
> *and share the truth from a Living Word.*

Lord, grant us simplicity of faith
and a yearning to share it,
in Your name we pray.
Amen.

Final Hymn

It is my wish that at the Requiem Mass to celebrate my passing
on to a new life that this wonderful song be sung.

O Lord my God when I in awesome wonder,
Consider all the worlds Thy hand has made,
I see the stars, I hear the rolling thunder,
Thy power throughout the universe displayed.
   Then sing my soul, my Saviour God to Thee:
   How great Thou art, how great Thou art.
   Then sings my soul, my Saviour God to Thee:
   How great Thou art, how great Thou art.
And when I think that God his Son not sparing,
Sent Him to die, I scarce can take it in
That on the cross, my burden gladly bearing,
He bled and died to take away my sin.
   Then sing my soul, my Saviour God to Thee:
   How great Thou art, how great Thou art.
   Then sings my soul, my Saviour God to Thee:
   How great Thou art, how great Thou art.
When Christ shall come with shout of acclamation
and lead me home, what joy shall fill my heart;
Then I shall bow in humble adoration,
   And there proclaim, My God, how great thou art.
   How great Thou art, how great Thou art
   Then sings my soul, my Saviour God to Thee:
   How great Thou art, how great Thou art.